Praise For
From Red to Black 2

In his latest work, From Red to Black 2, Robert Curry masterfully navigates another impressive business turnaround, this time set against the rugged backdrop of Utah. His hands-on involvement in reviving Utah Off-road, Inc., a business on the brink of collapse—serves as a gripping case study that is as instructive as it is entertaining.

What sets this book apart is the author's unfiltered voice and straight-shooting style. He calls it like it is, cutting through the fluff to deliver blunt assessments and actionable advice to the beleaguered owners, Suzanne and Jonathan. From reorganizing the shop layout to refining the owners' appearances and hiring competent staff, no issue is too big or too small for his scrutiny.

The most enlightening aspect of the book is the PIRs (Profit Improvement Recommendations). These tailored interventions make for an interesting read and offer valuable lessons in business management and problem-solving. They demonstrate the author's incredible acumen for reading between the lines, discerning the root problems that often elude even the most astute business owners.

'From Red to Black 2' is more than just a turnaround story; it's a masterclass in confronting the uncomfortable, shedding light on what it truly takes to bring a failing business back from the brink. This book is a must-read for entrepreneurs, managers, and anyone interested in the real-world mechanics of business rescue.

—Anne E. Beall, PhD,
CEO of Beall Research
& Award-Winning Author

THE FOURTH BOOK IN THE 'FROM LOSSES TO PROFITS' SERIES

FROM RED

TO
BLACK 2

ROBERT S. CURRY

BUSINESS RECOVERY SPECIALIST

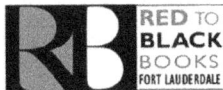

RED TO
BLACK
BOOKS
FORT LAUDERDALE

DISCLAIMER: THIS BOOK IS DESIGNED TO PROVIDE ACCURATE and authoritative information regarding the subject matter covered. The publisher and author are not engaged in rendering legal advice or any other professional services to the reader. If legal advice or other assistance is required, the services of a competent professional should be sought. The reader should be aware that laws and rules applicable to their situation may differ from the information in this book. It is the responsibility of the reader to seek professional guidance whenever necessary. The author and publisher are not responsible for any adverse effects or consequences resulting from the use of the information in this book.

THE MATTER OF UTAH OFF-ROAD, INC. IS BASED ON A REAL CLIENT. However, actual names and identifying characteristics have not been used, and any resemblance to a specific individual or company is coincidental.

PUBLISHED BY:
RED TO BLACK BOOKS
FORT LAUDERDALE, FLORIDA

COPYRIGHT © 2024 BY ROBERT S. CURRY

ISBN-13: 978-1-7327891-0-4

LIBRARY OF CONGRESS CONTROL NUMBER: 2017947347

PRINTED IN THE UNITED STATES OF AMERICA

*To my wife, Esther Curry—
my best friend, partner, lover,
advisor, and supporter.*

CONTENTS

PREFACE

I HAVE WRITTEN AND PUBLISHED THREE BOOKS in my "From Losses To Profits" series. This book is my fourth. All four books are stories about financial turnarounds that I have done for actual unprofitable companies. I authored these books in a case study or storytelling format. Each book talks about the fundamental problem areas of a client's business. Then, I will describe how I resolved the problems that generated profits for the company. The four books discuss the company's main characters (the owners, management teams, and key employees). Next is the company's financial and operational problem areas, which I found during the consulting engagement. The clients were losing money in my prior three books, From Red to Black, The Turnaround, and The Turnaround 2. They were close to filing for bankruptcy protection before the turnaround consulting engagement started. The owners and management teams needed to learn how to stop the company from losing money. Each owner hired me to review the details of their company to identify the problems. My job was to help them make the necessary changes to turn the business around From Losses to Profits.

The most significant areas of my books are the findings, documenting, and resolving each problem area of a client's business. Each business has had a unique combination of problems that caused the companies to lose money. I have always documented all the issues in writing when working with the client. I have used an observation, conclusion, action plan, and financial benefit format. After finding each problem, I create a list of the steps to implement the best business practice solutions or action plans to resolve all the issues. By documenting all the problems in the company, I have in writing all the issues that I need to change, adjust, or fix. These Profit Improvement Recommendations, or "PIRs" provide me with a checklist or roadmap of all the areas in the company that I need to improve to be profitable.

Over my 25 years of doing turnarounds for more than 80 clients, I have always used this PIR system to aid me in helping my clients go From Losses to Profits. My goal during my turnaround consulting engagements has always been to upgrade the overall performance of the business leader and management team. By doing this, it also improves the financial and operating results of the business.

With each book, I have changed the clients' names to protect the confidentiality of the companies, owners, and employees.

My goal for each book is to share the problems and weaknesses in each of my client's businesses with the readers. I then explain to the readers the resolution of each company's issues. Next, I describe the action steps necessary to resolve the problems and issues. Finally, I estimate the financial gain to the company after we fix the problems.

I have highlighted the PIRs and the operational and financial forms in every chapter. I aim for the readers to easily find the best practice information after reading the book. These forms, reports, policies, and procedures have helped my clients' companies remain profitable after we complete the turnaround engagement. I intend for each book's readers to identify with the problem areas for each of my turnaround clients. Then, the readers can use the problem-solving information to improve the management and performance of their own company. With all the information in my four books, the readers can use the PIRs to enhance their company's success. They can do it without hiring a Turnaround Specialist like my clients have had to do by hiring me.

My first book, From Red to Black, a Business Turnaround, is about a company in Florida named ABC Hurricane Shutters. This company had more sales than they could manufacture and install. Their high-demand products were hurricane shutters. Most companies that have strong demand for their products are very profitable. Unfortunately, because of the weak management team, this client could not manufacture and install the hurricane shutters fast enough. This problem caused the company to lose money three years in a row. When you read the book, you will find that several other problems and issues put the company in a negative cash flow status.

After the turnaround, the company became very profitable once we terminated the weak managers and fired the non-productive employees. We replaced them with a strong management team and hardworking employees. The productivity of the manufacturing and installation departments under the new management improved materially in weeks. These simple changes caused the company's annual sales to double. Their financial results went From Losses to Profits.

My second book, The Turnaround, is about the company in Pennsylvania - ABC Computer Distributors. This company sells computer hardware, software, and services. This company needed to improve the computer sales and service departments. Their problems were due to its weak management team, which included its owner. In the year before the turnaround, the business lost approximately (-$850,000) on $48,000,000 of sales.

I implemented the best business practices in the sales and service departments during the turnaround engagement. The best practices included weekly sales training meetings for the whole sales department. The sessions were on Friday afternoons. When I started the turnaround engagement, at least half of the salespeople would travel to the New Jersey shore. They would enjoy a long, relaxing weekend on the beach from Thursday night to Sunday. By holding the mandatory sales meetings on Friday afternoons, I had confidence that the salespeople were now working at least a 40-hour workweek. This change included working every Thursday and Friday. I aimed to motivate each salesperson to improve their sales production, which worked!

You will notice we added other sales policies and procedures when you read the book. The goal was to help motivate the sales department to become more productive with each salesperson's daily and weekly sales efforts.

During the actual turnaround, the company's sales grew from $48,000,000 during the prior 12 months to $130,000,000 in the first nine months of the engagement. I am quoting the sales total for only nine months because we sold the company due to receiving a purchase offer to sell the company that was too good to turn down. We ended the turnaround by closing the sale of the company at a substantial premium.

The Turnaround 2, the Matter of ABC Off-road Supply Company, is my third book in the From Losses to Profits series. It is a true story about an offroad supply company in Utah with $6,300,000 in annual sales. The business had lost money the prior two years before the owners hired me to improve the company's profit performance.

During the turnaround engagement, the company's sales grew from $6,300,000 to over $13,000,000 the year during my consulting engagement. The reward to the two owners was a substantial increase in their cash flow. The owner's compensation also grew from the material growth of the company's sales and profits.

This fourth book is about one of my recent turnarounds of a company in the offroad manufacturing business. They manufactured mostly offroad bumpers for their customers. The owners, a husband-and-wife team, started the company in 2004. Utah Off-road, Inc. ("Utah Off-road") began as a research and design business to develop new innovative offroad equipment. By 2005, the company had introduced a new series of bumpers and tire carrier systems. Their next goal was to put their focus on becoming a full-fledged manufacturer of premium offroad equipment. The company has continued to expand its product lines, offering more offroad options for SUVs, jeeps, and pickup trucks.

I hope the readers of this book, and my other three books in the From Losses to Profits series, enjoy the stories in each book. I also hope the readers learn new things about business that they can now use in their own company. Unfortunately, being able to find "cash-draining problems" in your own company is usually a challenging task. It is much easier for an outside consultant to see the problems and the solutions. This is typically true because other people are looking at the issues with a fresh set of eyes.

As you read this book, please be aware that I am trying to share more information about turning a company around From Losses to Profits than an exciting story about an offroad equipment manufacturer. The company owners in this book made me aware that many business owners of small to medium-sized companies need help from a turnaround specialist to make their company profitable. If they don't get the support, they will crash and burn. Even though I have worked with 80-plus companies, I have always continued to learn new stuff. The story in this book is an excellent example of a client I learned a lot from!

INTRODUCTION

*"The way to get started is to
quit talking and begin doing."*
– WALT DISNEY – AN AMERICAN ANIMATOR,
FILM PRODUCER AND ENTREPRENEUR

SINCE I GRADUATED FROM COLLEGE, I HAVE always wondered why some businesses are so remarkably successful (Amazon, Microsoft, Apple, etc.) and why others fail miserably. That question has stayed with me to this day. Only when I started running companies as the president/ CEO of the organization, doing turnarounds, writing, and publishing three books (soon to be four) on the topic did I have a more comprehensive understanding of the answer to my successful business question. A business to be successful requires different essential elements to be profitable. Below is a 30,000-foot overview of a successful business' crucial requirements. These elements include:

1. A strong leader (this is by far the most crucial element),

2. A professional management team,

3. Quality products or services with a good demand by the public,

4. Positive cash flow from operations,

5. A solid cash flow management process,

6. Timely accurate financial and operational reporting,

7. A business plan and operating budget to help guide the business through the current and future years,

8. Disciplined hiring policies for managers and employees,

9. Excellent communication between the leader, the management team, and the employees,

10. Strong relationships with the company's customers, vendors/suppliers, and their financial institution,

11. Strong systems, controls, policies, and procedures ensure efficient use of the company's assets and employees.

12. A marketing program that communicates well with the company's existing and potential customers.

My first promotion to president was when I was the chief financial officer working for a $100,000,000 homebuilder-developor in Pennsylvania. The two owners (Hal and Nick) hired me. At that time, the two owners assumed the company's leadership as co-presidents and successfully managed the business.

The business had eight homebuilding developments active under construction, all in the Philadelphia area. Each construction site had a general manager overseeing sales and building the homes. The company's management and staff were the most solid of any company that I have ever worked for or worked with as a turnaround specialist since then. One key factor about this company that made it so successful was that there was no employee turnover of the management or staff before and after I joined the organization. The CFO position was only vacant because the prior gentleman holding the CFO title was in an automobile accident and died. I remember that very few employees left the company during the eight years I led this organization, two years as the CFO and six years as the president. Whenever an employee left the company, it was usually because of retirement.

After being the CFO for two years, Hal and Nick promoted me to run the company because they both wanted to move into semi-retirement, play golf, and enjoy their families. During the two years of working directly for those two gentlemen, I learned how to lead their company using their quality management style.

Hal and Nick had a straightforward business philosophy that defined their management style, which made the company so successful for years and years.

"The way to make money in business is to hire the best people in the area, treat them with respect, give them the tools to do their job, provide them an excellent environment to work in, and compensate them fairly."

This statement was the foundation of their success in the homebuilding business. The truth is that the information in this statement would make any company successful if the leader and management team followed this simple business philosophy. These two gentlemen lived by this business philosophy and hired people (managers and employees) who also lived by the same philosophical statement.

I learned a lot from Hal and Nick. They have proved invaluable in my professional training as a senior executive and turnaround specialist. They used other successful policies and procedures in their business that caused the company's management and employees never to leave. Hal and Nick's business skills, as listed below, helped to maximize their success:

1. Their leadership skills were the best when supervising the executive team, employees, suppliers/vendors, and, very importantly, the customers.

2. They treated every employee with respect 100% of the time.

3. Their hiring practice for all employees was very consistent. They have yet to "settle" for a candidate for a position within the company. Over the years of managing their successful business, they waited until they found the perfect candidate for the open position before considering hiring the person.

4. The two owners bonused all the managers and employees 25% of the company's profits yearly. During the years that I workod thorc, thc profit bonus to the employees was substantial because the company was so profitable!

This book is another story about one of my recent consulting engagements, a company located in Utah. Brian, the owner of ABC Off-road Supply, is the business owner discussed in my third book, The Turnaround 2. Brian introduced me to the two owners of Utah Off-road.

I hope that you enjoy the book!

Chapter 1

THE CLIENT REFERRAL

"The way to make money in business is to hire the best people in the area, treat them with respect, give them the tools to do their job, provide them an excellent environment to work in and compensate them fairly."
— HAROLD DAVIS, AMERICAN BUSINESSMAN, AND REAL ESTATE ENTREPRENEUR

Saturday, August 6th

IT WAS A VERY WARM AUGUST EVENING IN FORT Lauderdale when I received a phone call from the owner of my most recent turnaround client in Utah, Brian from ABC Off-road Supply. Brian is one of my all-time favorite clients, so getting his call was a pleasant surprise. We chatted briefly about his business and how its sales have grown by over 100% since I was there a year ago for the turnaround engagement. I was so happy to hear the great news because Brian works hard and deserves the best. It is beautiful to hear that his challenging work is paying off with the success of his business.

Then Brian told me he has recently been talking to friends who own an aftermarket offroad manufacturing company. The name of his friend's business is Utah Off-road. I printed the company's name in my notebook to research his friend's business later. Brian said that his friend's company has recently been struggling. He told me he talked to them about how I helped his company turn around and go From Losses to Profits! Brian's friends, Jonathan and Suzanne, asked him if he would give me a call to see if I was available to come to Utah right now. Jonathan wanted to know if I would be interested in a turnaround consulting engagement for his company as I did with ABC Off-road Supply. Brian told his friend that he would give me a call because he wanted to talk to me about another critical issue.

Before discussing his friend, Jonathan, and his business, I asked Brian what is the issue he wanted to discuss with me. Brian recently received three phone calls from three different investment bank organizations interested in buying his company. He told me that one of the parties said their firm was interested in rolling up companies in the offroad supply and manufacturing industry. I asked Brian if he knew Jonathan's company was also on this roll-up list. Brian said, "Yes, it is."

Brian then told me a story about an investment bank he was familiar with that was acquiring smaller businesses in the offroad industry. He said that the acquired companies crashed and burned briefly after the acquisition. Brian said that the investment bank that bought the companies needed to pay more attention to these new businesses. The acquired businesses' sales crashed, and so did the profits. That was one of the problems, but the bigger problem was a significant percentage of key employees jumped ship after the acquisition and went to work for their competitors. If your company loses a couple of talented salespeople and managers in this offroad industry or any industry, the company will spiral down very quickly.

I politely interrupted Brian because I had to tell him a story he needed to hear and understand. The issue is that there is a great deal of exposure when an owner is considering selling his business. Brian had never sold a company before, so he was naïve to the issue and at risk.

My wife was the president of a five-campus medical college for a long time in Florida. We decided it was time to sell the college and retire about two years ago. The only person we discussed selling the college was our corporate attorney, who promised to keep our intentions to sell the college a secret. My wife's management team (12 executives) worked for her and the college for a minimum of 13 years and a maximum of 28 years. The loyalty of the executive team to my wife was exceptional. The college was remarkably successful financially, and the education delivered to the students was the best.

We kept the potential sale of the college a secret from everyone involved in the college business. We were concerned that the managers would look for new jobs and leave the college if they knew my wife would not be the senior executive after the sale, and we were right.

Our attorney knew someone interested in buying a college in Florida and introduced us to the individual. The potential buyer toured the five campus buildings three times each. He also did due diligence on the college's financial records. Finally, the executives who reported to my wife on the management team started asking questions about who the guy was visiting all the campus buildings. We knew that we could not lie to the managers about the situation. We knew that we had to tell them the truth. We realized that telling them the facts that the college was up for sale would put us and the college at risk. If we could not find a buyer for the college, the management team would assume the worst. They would all be out looking and finding new jobs. This problem would materially damage the business of the college financially and the quality of the education for the existing students.

To protect against this problem, we offered each manager a substantial financial stay bonus if the college still employed them for at least three months after the sale. The settlement date for the sale of the college was May 24th to the new owner. The buyer offered my wife a one-year consulting engagement to stay with the college to ensure the transition from my wife's management to the new senior executives went smoothly. The college paid the 12 executives the stay bonuses on August 24th.

Unfortunately, the managers' loyalty to my wife and the college did not transition to the new owner and his four managers in Brooklyn, New York. Within 60 days, all 12 managers gave notice and left the college for new jobs. Even though the new owner hired my wife as a consultant, the existing management team did not want to work for the new ownership for one day longer than they had to.

There used to be a radio personality in Chicago years ago named *Paul Harvey* who would tell heartfelt stories on the radio. As he would finish telling the story's last chapter, it would usually bring tears to my eyes. He would end every story with the statement: '*And now you know… the rest of the story.*'

Because of:

1. The loss of the existing management team,

2. The absentee owner and his managers in New York for a five-campus college in Florida,

3. The new owner's management style versus my wife's for her managers, the college business took a terrible turn from being very profitable to reducing sales and profits.

Within a year and a half, the college's student population dropped from 1,800 students on the day of the settlement to less than 500 students as of the date I authored this book. As one can imagine, the company will be in big trouble when any business' sales drop by 72%. The tears that I had in my eyes for the endings of *Paul Harvey's* stories are just like the tears that I have when I think of everything that my wife achieved with the college that has gone down the drain with the management of the new college owner. '*And now you know…the rest of the story*'… about the college with the new owner who bought the business.

When I told Brian this story, he had a severe tone in his voice and thanked me. Brian's whole net worth is his business, and he took the message of my story very seriously. He now understood one of the significant risks for a business owner associated with planning to sell his business.

Brian and I discussed this issue for a while. I asked Brian, "What would you do after you sold your business to one of these investment banks?" He said that he did not have a clue. He said, "Bob, I have all I can manage to keep my company profitable right now; I do not have time to solve hypothetical transactions. Bob, that is your job! And that includes helping my friend, Jonathan, with his business."

Brian seemed flattered that he was getting these phone calls from people interested in buying his company. I told him that if I were him, I would be a little concerned about the crash and burning results of the acquired businesses he described. Just a year and a half ago, his company was in severe financial trouble, and now he has people wanting to buy his business. Brian said, "Bob, I do not know what to do. I keep wondering if I should continue to run this business now that it is successful or sell it and get out. I am only 44 years old and not ready to retire!" He also said he was now paying himself and his partner big salaries from the profits. He is enjoying his new life with having enough money in the bank to live comfortably. I asked him, "If you are enjoying life now that your business is so successful, why do anything to change it?" He did not have a conclusive answer to my question. He said, "Bob, if I did have an answer to your question, I probably would not have called you!" I responded, "Brian, yes, you would have. You wanted to talk to me about your friend Jonathan and his business."

When I first met Brian, his business struggled to generate the funds to fund the bi-weekly payroll. Now, he is making more money than he ever dreamed about. Plus, there is still the opportunity for ABC Off-road Supply to grow and kick off more money for the two owners. I told Brian, "Now that your business is successful, do not try to fix it. You should enjoy life and start building up a large savings account to pay for your later-in-life expenses when you are too old to work and make any money."

Brian and I talked for about 30 minutes more about him considering selling the business or keeping it running and growing it to increase the company's future value. We decided to sit and chat about his options the next time I am in Utah. By then, he said that he would have more information about these people who were calling him, and then we could have a more intelligent conversation about the topic.

We then switched over and started talking about his friend Jonathan and the troubles with his business. Since Brian participated in the turnaround of ABC Off-road Supply, in his mind, he is now an expert in turning around a business. He explained that he knew what was wrong with Jonathan's company and why it was struggling.

Jonathan and his wife, Suzanne, own Utah Off-road, Inc., an aftermarket offroad bumper manufacturing company. The business is struggling like Brian's company was two years ago. Brian told me he discussed with Jonathan during a recent dinner meeting what I did to turn around his company. Brian recommended to Jonathan to immediately buy my three books, *From Red to Black*, *a Business Turnaround*, *The Turnaround*, and *The Turnaround 2*. He told Jonathan to read them before contacting me. Brian told Jonathan that if he follows his instructions about reading the From Losses to Profits series of books first, he will better understand why he needs the help of a turnaround specialist to fix his company. As of today, I wonder if Jonathan took Brian's advice about reading my books.

Brian told me all about his friend's business and explained why he believed that his business was struggling. Brian and I talked about Jonathan, Suzanne, and their company for another hour. Brian has known them for over ten years. Brian's and Jonathan's companies do business with each other from time to time. Brian asked if I had available time in my current schedule to visit with his friends to help them with their business. I told Brian that I could take on another client and for him to ask Jonathan and Suzanne to give me a call to discuss the issue.

The following day, around 11:00 a.m. EST (9:00 a.m. in Utah), my phone rang, and I noticed the call was coming from an area code in Utah. Sure enough, it was Brian's friend Jonathan calling to talk about his business that was struggling to make a profit. Jonathan and I spoke for over two hours about his offroad manufacturing business and all the problems he and his wife were experiencing. By the time we ended our conversation, I had 15 pages of notes I wrote while talking. I always take handwritten notes when talking to one of my clients or potential clients because I always want to remember everything. If I write notes during the conversation, I will always remember all the essential facts we discussed.

Jonathan is very long-winded when he starts talking to tell a story about his business. He is the type of person who could make a short story long and a long one even longer. Another thing about Jonathan is that he is intense about everything that he talks about. Also, while telling his story, he stops and asks questions like: "Are you still with me, Bob?" My usual answer: "Jonathan, I agree with you 100%!" But honestly, there are times that I do not know what he is talking about or what he is asking me. I am an excellent listener because that is how I learn things about my clients. But, if the conversation is going off on a tangent with nothing to do with the client's business, there are times that I check out of the conversation. That certainly happened with my first phone call with Jonathan.

At the end of our conversation, Jonathan asked, "Bob, are you going to be able to come to Utah and help us like you helped Brian at ABC Off-road Supply?" There was a long pause before I answered the question, primarily because I was considering whether I wanted to do another turnaround in Utah. Utah is a four-and-a-half to five-hour flight from Fort Lauderdale each way. Traveling clear across the United States for a job means a travel day on each trip to and from the consulting engagement. It is a day to get to the client's offices and a day to return home. I knew the routine well because my consulting with ABC Off-road Supply lasted nine months, so I made 18 flights to Utah and 18 flights home.

When I do a turnaround engagement, I am usually at the client's office for three days to one week. Then, I skip a week and visit the third week of the month. While talking to Jonathan, I could envision myself sitting on the airplane, traveling to Utah again. Finally, I answered Jonathan's question: "I will send you a proposal for the engagement. If you and Suzanne are comfortable with the terms and conditions of the agreement, sign it, scan it, and email me back a copy of the signed document." Thirty minutes after I sent him the consulting agreement, I received an email with the document attached with his and Suzanne's signature. I co-signed the signature page and emailed the fully executed contract back to Jonathan. So, I made my decision. I would make several more trips to and from Utah.

I was excited about accepting this new turnaround engagement. I love what I do for a living: turnarounds. However, I prefer to avoid traveling across the US to do consulting engagements. The redeeming feature of this deal is that my first trip to Utah will be in early August, when the weather in the Salt Lake City area will be good. It will be warm in Utah during the summer. My first trip to Utah for the ABC Off-road Supply engagement was in late November. When I got off the plane to start that engagement, it was about 20°

Fahrenheit with ten inches of snow on the ground and the wind blowing hard. Leaving Fort Lauderdale when the weather was 80° and landing in Salt Lake City when it was 20° was a challenging engagement to start. The temperature change hits me hard when it was 60° colder.

That afternoon, I booked the flight and hotel room to fly to Utah on Sunday to start the job on Monday morning. Jonathan told me he would pick me up at the airport and give me a Jeep to use for the week rather than me renting a car. I packed my suitcase on Saturday for the trip. When I woke up Sunday morning, I had to shower, dress for the weather in Utah, and have my wife take me to the airport in Fort Lauderdale. Saturday evening, I researched everything I could find out about the company online. I reviewed my notes from my earlier phone call with Jonathan, so I was well-prepared to start the job when I arrived Monday morning at the company's offices. I posted the handwritten notes on my computer, which I would use once I began the new consulting job on Monday.

On my five-hour flight from Fort Lauderdale to Utah, I did more research on the status of the offroad industry. I was concerned that the current Covid-19 pandemic would hurt their company and the aftermarket offroad industry.

When I landed in Utah, I got my suitcase at baggage claim and went outside to the passenger pickup area. I looked around for them, but Jonathan and Suzanne were not there. Ten minutes later, Suzanne texted me, stating they were running late and would arrive in 20 minutes. Finally, they drove up in their black Ford Bronco to take me to my hotel for the evening. The Bronco was all "blinged-up" with offroad aftermarket products. I had to walk completely around the vehicle to see what they had installed. The truck had huge front and back bumpers that made it look substantial. On the front bumper was a large winch mounted in the center. The back bumper had a dual tire carrier attached. On the roof of the vehicle was an Ultra Roof Rack. Also mounted above the front windshield was a row of six spotlights that looked like they could light up a football stadium. The ten-inch lift kit made the Bronco look substantial and high up. It had Satin Black KMC wheels and a fancy lug nut package. The massive tires and solid black wheels raised the vehicle even further to the point that once the door was open, I had to figure out how to get my body into the passenger seat without looking like I needed a ladder to help get me up there. Nothing I saw on the Bronco surprised me because there were a bunch of "blinged-up" offroad trucks at my last turnaround in Utah! But this was indeed an aftermarket offroad vehicle!

My first meeting with Jonathan and Suzanne was enjoyable. They are both genuinely lovely people. They are both in their early forties and have four children at home, ages from six to 17 years old. I got Jonathan's *Reader Digest* version of their company as we drove to my hotel. Early in my relationship with these owners, I learned that Jonathan is the talker, and Suzanne is a good listener while Jonathan is talking.

Jonathan told me that he has known Brian for a long time since he started his company, ABC Off-road Supply. He said Brian was extremely hyper until a year and a half ago. Jonathan said, "Suzanne and I would meet Brian for dinner from time to time. Bob, usually, Brian was so stressed out about his company that he would not finish his dinner before he rushed off. Now, meeting with Brian is different. Since you helped him improve his business to be very profitable, he is a vastly different person. Bob, I asked Brian for your phone number because I want you to come to our company and do the same for us that you did for ABC Off-road Supply."

Suzanne said, "And Bob, what did you do to get Brian to settle down and enjoy life? Please do the same with Jonathan! If you can do that, it would be a miracle!" I just laughed and thought about how Suzanne must suffer or have the perfect pharmaceutical prescription to cope with the daily stressful issue of dealing with Jonathan!

On the trip to my hotel, we agreed to meet for breakfast the following morning so they could give me a complete company history from the day they started the company until the current date.

Chapter 2

THE BREAKFAST MEETING

"You only have to do a few things right in your life so long as you don't do too many things wrong."
— WARREN BUFFETT – AN AMERICAN BUSINESS MAGNATE, INVESTOR AND PHILANTHROPIST

Monday, August 7th – Day 1 of week 1 of the turnaround engagement

AT 8:00 A.M., MONDAY MORNING, JONATHAN, Suzanne, and I were to meet at the restaurant in my hotel for breakfast. I dressed early to get to the restaurant at least 15 minutes before the meeting just in case my clients showed up early. I received a text message from Suzanne at 8:20 a.m. (20 minutes late) saying they were running late. She texted me, saying they should be at the restaurant in ten minutes. Per her text, they ran 30 minutes late because they had trouble getting their four kids out of bed. She was preparing a healthy breakfast and had to drop them all off at their respective schools. Since it was late August, the summer was over for the kids. Today was their first day at school. I reconciled this by remembering what it was like for my mother to get me, my four sisters, and my brother off to school each morning while growing up. I am sure Suzanne getting their four kids off to school each morning is quite a task!

As you read this book, you will note at various times that the earliest Jonathan and Suzanne showed up for a meeting was at least 25 minutes later than they promised. It is funny. Some people must work hard to break their poor habits of constantly being late for meetings. My father always used to say:

> *"There are no good excuses for being late for a meeting. It always leaves a good impression on the other people attending the meeting when you arrive on time! Being late, I do not have to explain that! No one enjoys waiting patiently for the other party to show up finally!"*

At my first turnaround engagement in Utah, I learned that the owners of companies in the offroad industry dress very casually at work. That was certainly the case with Jonathan and Suzanne. Their work attire was a company-logoed tee shirt and shorts or capris. They were both wearing black work boots and black socks. I could not tell if they were the company's owners or if they both worked in the shop as welders based on how they dressed. I have always believed that the image of how the business owner or management team dresses reflects a clear image of how they respect their business. It is much more than just how they dress. The company will suffer if the owners do not demand their managers and employees dress professionally. It is the same with keeping their offices, manufacturing areas, retail showrooms, and company vehicles looking clean and organized. If the owners do not respect the business, neither will their managers or employees. When that is the case, the owners should hire a turnaround specialist. My clients signed a consulting agreement for me to support them in cleaning up the business and making it profitable.

Jonathan and Suzanne reminded me of an old client during this first face-to-face meeting. The client, ABC Commercial Roofing, was owned by Alan Roth. The company was in Maine. These two owners in Utah had about the same or less business knowledge and experience as Alan. Both companies' owners needed to learn how to manage a successful business.

A side note about that turnaround in Maine: Thank goodness the consulting engagement started in early May. I would only have accepted the turnaround job if it were to begin sometime between the middle of April and the beginning of July. I can deal with the weather when it is cold. But in Maine, from November until the middle of March, it is freezing in that state. I love living in Florida, where it is warm 12 months a year, so I can play golf whenever I want to and not freeze to death!

It was in a big old building when I arrived at the company's facility in Lewiston, Maine. I went into the company's main entrance and told the receptionist I was there to meet with the owner, Alan Roth. The receptionist introduced herself as Shelly and immediately asked me to follow her to their conference room. She said that Alan was going to meet me there. I sat at the conference room table. Shelly asked me if I would like a hot cup of coffee. In Maine, everyone drinks a lot of hot coffee to keep themselves warm. The reason, it is always cold there! A minute later, Shelly brought me a hot cup of coffee and a pitcher of cream. I thanked her, and she said that Alan would join me soon. She said he was on a phone call with one of the company's customers.

Five minutes later, a guy looking like the company's janitor walked into the conference room with his hot cup of coffee. He extended his right hand to shake hands. This gentleman wore an old pair of jeans, a flannel shirt, and dirty work boots. He had long blonde hair that hung down below his collar with bangs that touched the top rim of his glasses. His mustache looked like he had not trimmed it in a month. Alan was in his early forties.

I am sure I looked very puzzled when he looked at me. I was expecting to meet with Alan Roth, the owner/president of ABC Commercial Roofing. I was unsure why a guy who looked like the company's janitor was shaking my hand. Alan said, "Bob Curry, I am Alan Roth, the owner and president of ABC Commercial Roofers." I tried to control the surprised look on my face, but I failed miserably. I tried to restrain myself. I did not want Alan to fire me from the consulting engagement before I started.

Alan and I spent the whole morning in the conference room. From his point of view, we discussed what was wrong with his company. He did not know why it was losing money every month. Alan had a list of notes that he had prepared for our meeting. I was impressed with Alan, who seemed like a meticulous, intelligent young man. While wearing his old jeans and flannel shirt, his image did not match the intelligence of this business owner. The owner who was sitting across the conference room table from me discussing his commercial roofing company is a bright guy. The conflict between how he dressed for our meeting and who he was, the owner/president of a $20,000,000 commercial roofing company, did not match my mental image of him before we first met.

At noon, Shelly entered the conference room and asked Alan if she should order lunch for us. Alan looked at me to see if I was interested in having lunch there and continuing our conversation about his company. I said: "Sure!" I told Shelly I would enjoy a nice salad with honey mustard dressing. Alan told Shelly that he would have his usual, whatever that was. She nodded her head yes and disappeared to order our lunch.

By then, I had at least 20 pages of handwritten notes about our conversation. One of my notes was that I had to discuss with Alan about upgrading his image. In other words, in the future, he dresses like the owner / president of a $20,000,000 company.

Twenty minutes later, Shelly returned with our lunch and set up the food while we talked. I put my pen down and moved my notes off to the side to eat my salad and drink a bottle of water. Alan had a giant cheeseburger, a huge plate of French fries, and a Coke.

After Alan had taken a couple of bites of his burger, he asked me a question. "So, Bob, what is the most important problem from everything we discussed this morning? What would you first work on at the beginning of this turnaround?" With Alan's question, he opened the door. This was now my opportunity to answer him about how he dresses daily at his commercial roofing company. I first considered how Alan would react if I commented about his clothes, shoes, and hairstyle. I decided to roll the dice and be very frank with my comments.

I said, "Alan, you will be surprised by my answer to your question! Even though we have just met each other this morning for the first time, I trust you will not take offense to what I am going to tell you. Alan, I do not like how you dress to represent the leader of this company. Your wardrobe makes you look like you are the janitor for the company, not the owner/president. Every day you come to work, your managers, employees, customers, vendors, and bankers should see you as a strong, intelligent business leader. All those people should look at you daily and say, "I trust and respect Alan, and I will follow him anywhere, anytime!" To get that kind of respect from your people, you must both look and act the part. This company is important to many, many people. Your managers and employees depend on your leadership because their paychecks are how they care for and feed their families. They must be able to look at you and trust that you are making good business decisions that will make this company very profitable. All your employees must trust that their jobs and families are secure while working for your company. They want to be able to look at you and say: "My job and my family are safe because you, Alan, are leading this great company! Alan, how you dress today sends the exact opposite message to your managers and employees!"

"So, Bob," Alan asked, "How do you suggest I fix this problem?" I answered Alan's question after I took a deep breath of fresh air. I was pleased with how he received my comments about his current work wardrobe. "Alan, as soon as we finish this conversation, you call your wife from your office. You tell her you will take her out to dinner tonight. And then, after the two of you finish your meal, you will take her to the local department store. She will help you upgrade the clothes you wear to work every day in the future. It would be best if you had her pick out at least five or six nice pairs of khakis. She should also pick out six or seven professional dress shirts and a couple of new work boots."

"Then, after the two of you finish wardrobe shopping, your next stop will be at the barbershop. That is where you will get a professional business haircut. Alan, you can only leave the barber's chair once your wife approves your haircut. Your hair is too long for the owner/president of a $20,000,000 roofing company. When you come to work tomorrow with your new business outfit and professional-looking haircut, things here are going to be different. I promise your employees will look at the changes and treat you entirely differently than they do today. You are going to be the receptor of a whole new level of respect as the president of this company."

As I finished my little speech, I looked at Alan and held my breath. I was hoping he would not fire me on the spot for being disrespectful to him on the first half day I was at my client's facilities.

Much to my surprise, Alan had a big smile on his face. I asked Alan why he was smiling. Alan said, "Bob, I do not know if you are aware of the history of this company. My father started ABC Commercial Roofing over 40 years ago. My dad was an "old school" type of guy and treated all the employees here disrespectfully. He also treated me, his only son, the same way. The last thing I wanted to do was treat the company's employees like my father did. While he was running the company, he shared nothing with me. He rarely talked to me during working hours. A couple of years ago, I asked him what his succession plans were for the company, and he refused to answer me. Yes, Bob, before you ask, no one liked my father. He did not discriminate. He disrespected everyone, including the managers, employees, customers, suppliers, and vendors. The company was profitable for many years because no commercial roofing companies were within 100 miles of Lewiston."

"Over the years, I have talked with my wife about leaving the company and finding a new job. I created a resume and was ready to mail it to the local job openings. One night, two years ago, I was home in my office working, and my phone rang. The call was from the local hospital. My dad had a heart attack that evening and died that night. My mother died five years ago, and I do not have any siblings. I was the only family member alive when my dad passed, so it suddenly became my responsibility to run this company with zero management experience."

"So, Bob, as you are aware, I have found that the position of owner/president is the loneliest job in the world! That sounds weird, but it is true. This company needs a board of directors but has never had one. That is because no one liked my father enough to be a board member. The issue was mutual with my father; no one liked him, and he had no friends. Since my mother passed, Dad would go to work for eight hours and return home after work. No one would see him in the evenings or weekends. He hibernated, especially in winter when the temperature outside ranged between -20° and 0°."

"I cannot discuss the problems with the company with any of the managers. They report to me, and I do not want them to think I am, or the company is vulnerable. I cannot talk to my wife about the company problems because she knows nothing about the roofing business." Alan continued, "Bob, I have had zero business education or training on how to run this company ever since my dad passed. My management style is "trial and error!" This company has grown almost 50% since my father passed and has outgrown my trial-and-error management style. Even though our sales are growing, the company is still losing money monthly, and I am trying to figure out why. As you can guess, I hired you to clean up the company and teach me how to manage this business profitably. You probably have figured that out before we had this little discussion."

Alan continued, "So, Bob, I heard you loud and clear – Go to my office and call my wife. Invite her out to dinner and then go shopping and get a haircut. She will become my new fashion consultant and the person who approves of how I wear my hair in the future. So, should we call this meeting today My First Management Training Session? Bob, my wife, is going to love you for this. She has the same opinion as you about how I dress and wear my hair." Alan and I spent the rest of the afternoon together sharing information about his company.

On Tuesday morning, I got up and had a quick breakfast with a hot coffee at my hotel. I drove to my client's office and arrived promptly at 8:00 a.m.. After I parked my car, I entered the company's reception area. Shelly got out of her seat and came over to me with a massive smile. She gave me a big hug, one that I did not expect. Shelly said: "Bob, I hope that you don't mind me giving you a big hug. After you did what you did yesterday, I could not stop myself from giving you that great big hug." I wondered what I did yesterday that earned me that kind of affection. Shelly said, "Hurry and follow me, Bob. They are all waiting for you!" I had yet to learn what she was talking about. I followed Shelly down the hallway to the conference room. Shelly opened the door, and Alan and his whole management team were in the conference room. Alan jumped out of his seat when I entered the room. He extended his right hand to shake hands. After we shook hands, Alan said he wanted to introduce me to his management team. They were all seated at the table. The seven managers stood up and waited for Alan to introduce them to me. Alan introduced each manager and told me a little about their position with the company and their background. I noticed something when they all stood up. Every person was wearing a new pair of khakis, a brand-new long-sleeved collared shirt, and a new pair of shoes, each with a beautiful shine.

"Bob, after our meeting yesterday, I loved your idea about upgrading my wardrobe. So did my wife when I called her per your instructions. We both enjoyed it so much that I called a brief management meeting at the end of the day. At the meeting, I told everyone I was going to dinner with my wife. They were all invited and should bring their wives. At the restaurant during dinner, we all discussed your idea about dressing at work to look more like professionals. Everyone at this table agreed, and more importantly, our wives were enthusiastic about the wonderful change. Last night, the company treated the management team and their wives to dinner. The company also treated everyone on the management team to a wardrobe upgrade at the department store. I did not mention anything about going to the barbershop to my managers. I was the only one in the group who needed a haircut. I know the company is currently losing money. I decided to invest the company's funds in this wardrobe upgrade!

We also chose to have Shelly design new logoed company shirts for everyone. Everyone loved the idea, especially Shelly. Shelly has my permission to get on the internet to purchase high-quality white long-sleeve work shirts. The shirts will have our company's logo embroidered over the pocket. I looked around the conference room table at the management team. They all had their new outfits that they purchased last night. They all had big smiles on their faces. It was like they all had just found a $1,000 bill on the floor under each of their chairs.

The turnaround of the ABC Commercial Roofers was a fantastic success. The company became very profitable in the next three months. Alan's personality changed with his upgraded wardrobe and his new haircut. These two changes created a whole new image for him and the business. This story's moral is to always present yourself professionally, or more plainly stated, Dress for Success. Doing this will give you and your company better financial returns than expected. As *Paul Harvey* always says at the end of his radio talk shows – '*And now you know… the rest of the story!*'

I have shared this story with the readers of this book. The reason is similar issues hurt the owner of ABC Commercial Roofers and the owners of Utah Off-road.

Both companies had a huge morale problem with the managers and employees. The problem started with the owners of each company and hemorrhaged down to every employee in the company. At ABC Commercial Roofers, when Alan decided to dress for work looking like the janitor of the organization, he sent a silent message to the rest of the company. The message was, 'It is okay for everyone to come to work, look like a slob, and not care about the company's success.' Addressing Alan's wardrobe problem on the first day of the consulting engagement fixed the company's morale problem. Fixing the morale problem snowballed and resulted in fixing other organizational issues. The owner and management team resolved a documented list of topics without my involvement.

The morale problems for this client were like the ones at ABC Commercial Roofing. However, the difference, I thought, was that the two owners of this client were too far gone. They did not want to own and manage their company anymore. They just wanted to sell the company, put the proceeds from the sale in the bank, and do something else to make a living. *(See PIR #1 on page #44.)*

*   *   *

Whenever I am involved with a turnaround engagement with a client and discover a problem, I document the issue with a Profit Improvement Recommendation or PIR form (*See the actual PIR form on page #35.*). The PIR reports the problems in an observation, conclusion, action plan, and financial benefit format.

I also rate the problems on a one to ten basis. A one means minimal negative financial and cash flow impact for the company. It is not a senior priority to stop everything and focus on fixing the issue. On the other hand, a rating of ten means a material monetary and negative cash flow impact on the company caused by the problem. A problem with a rating of ten is a different story. I need to focus on the issue immediately to stop the bleeding of the cash out of the company. Over the years, this rating system has helped me a lot with turnarounds. I focus on the problems that need immediate attention to resolve and keep the money in the company. Also noted on the PIR form are the department executive, the responsible person, and the task deadline. Adding this information to the document helps to make those people accountable for solving the problem within the time noted on the PIR. My job as a turnaround consultant is to improve the cash flow and profits of the company. Focusing on material problems and fixing them as quickly as possible helps the company to go From Losses to Profits!

CEO Results Coaching
CRC

Profit Improvement Recommendation ("PIR")

PIR #	Department Executive	Company
Person Responsible	Task Deadline	PIR Rating

Observation:

Conclusion:

Action Plan:

Benefit Calculation:

Three-Year Benefit:

Sr. Consultant: _Robert S. Curry_____

Date _____

Client: _Utah Offroad, Inc._____

Signature: _____

            Senior Consultant

Signature: _____

            Client

(To the readers of this book - The PIR form and procedure, with a few simple modifications to the form, is an excellent system for documenting a problem in your own department or company. PIRs establish a plan to fix the issues and make people accountable for the problems and solutions.)

When my two new clients arrived at the restaurant for our breakfast meeting, I stood up to shake their hands. Standing up felt good because I waited for them sitting on a hard wooden chair for about 45 minutes. My butt was getting sore.

Jonathan is about five foot nine inches tall, has brown hair, a medium build, wears glasses, and is a good-looking young man. He has a well-trimmed beard. Suzanne is five foot eight inches tall with short brown hair down to the bottom of her ears. She is an attractive lady with a medium build and does not have a well-trimmed beard.

I learned from our conversation that Suzanne had not gained any business experience before joining the company. Her education was in social services. She worked for years as a counselor in a drug rehab clinic.

Suzanne's daily duties for the company are to manage the complete front end of the business. That includes accounting and financial reporting, accounts payable, and accounts receivables. It also includes human resources, vendor/supplier relations, marketing, website maintenance, customer services, and cash management. When I wrote this list of Suzanne's responsibilities on my notepad, I knew there would be significant problems with the front end of the business. No one person could manage and control all those responsibilities by herself, especially since she had no prior business experience. Suzanne has an employee, Karla, who recently had surgery on both of her knees and missed work more than she worked. Suzanne also had two employees who worked in the customer service department responsible for taking phone calls and emails from customers regarding their orders. Unfortunately, both employees were newcomers to the customer service department. Because of poor productivity in the company's shop, there was a six-month backlog of customer orders. In other words, if a customer wanted to order an offroad bumper for the front and back of their vehicle on February 1st, the customer would receive their bumpers on August 1st. The customer service department would receive customer complaints daily from customers who are not receiving their orders. About 15% of the customers would eventually cancel their order.

Jonathan was responsible for the rest of the business. That meant supervising the shop, which he hated to do. Jonathan's sweet spot was designing new offroad products. He designed mostly new bumpers for the new vehicles released by the car manufacturers annually.

Based upon my 25 years of doing turnarounds, having two inexperienced people in business managing a $3,200,000 company is a recipe for total failure. It is good that I was aware of these facts early in the consulting engagement. Knowing his weak business management skills helped me during the beginning of the consulting engagement. I knew I needed to look at everything that needed resolving!

Jonathan and Suzanne are married and have four children. Jonathan told me that he ruined his oldest son's high school years because he never pushed him into sports so he could be the starting quarterback on the football team. Jonathan described himself as being a computer nerd years ago when he was in high school. Their 17-year-old son, Bill, is also a gamer. He plans to go to college next year to study to be a computer programmer. Jonathan also told me that when he is not designing new offroad products at home for his company, he watches old movies and plays video games, just like his four children. I confessed to him that I knew nothing about the video games that a 45-year-old man or a 17-year-old gamer would play. The truth is, I do not watch old movies either.

As Jonathan and Suzanne sat down, the waiter approached our table to wait on us. Both owners ordered an omelet with everything but mushrooms, no potatoes, bacon, wheat toast, strawberry jelly, and a glass of water. It was easy for me to remember because they ordered the same food every time we had breakfast together. During the consulting engagement, we had breakfast together 18 times. I usually order a ham omelet with cheese and wheat toast! I also asked the server to please freshen my coffee!

The three of us sat at the breakfast table and talked for almost three hours, yes, three hours. About half of our discussion was about the company I am consulting with to grow and make it profitable. The other 50% of our conversations were about the economy and the current political situation. Jonathan also talked about today's prime interest rate and how booming the economy would be in the next two years because of the COVID-19 pandemic. Jonathan could speak nonstop about any subject, and I mean any topic. He believes he is an expert on any issue discussed during our conversations.

Before our meeting, I developed a comprehensive list of questions I wanted to ask and get answers from the two owners about their company. My goal was to get valuable information from them as soon as possible. I wanted to start the turnaround engagement with a complete understanding of their business named Utah Off-road. But the problem was when I asked a question, the conversation would veer off to other topics I had no interest in discussing and wasting our valuable time together. When applicable, I would write notes about the company, but never about Jonathan's opinion about the current economy or the other topics he would introduce during our conversations.

While sitting at breakfast that morning, I learned that Jonathan studied engineering in college and was extraordinarily intelligent. He designs the bumpers at his home in the evenings on his computer. I gathered from our conversations that Jonathan enjoys creating offroad bumpers because it is fun for him. He says he loves designing the company's products and hates managing the employees. Jonathan is obviously not a "people friendly" type of person.

About 90% of the time Jonathan talked, he would stare at his wife, Suzanne, and rarely look at me. I did not understand why he would not make eye contact with me during our conversations. She would slip in a one-word answer 'yea' to Jonathan's self-conversation when possible.

The next topic of our conversation was a company owner in Wisconsin. This owner was interested in buying Utah Off-road. The business owner of The Wisconsin Group has been teasing Jonathan and Suzanne for over three years that his company is interested in buying their company.

As he talked about this opportunity to sell his company, his voice got louder and louder. Jonathan was enthusiastic about this deal to sell his company. I looked into Jonathan's eyes, and they were excited. The excitement in his eyes was because he and Suzanne were both physically and emotionally exhausted from running the business and trying to raise their four children at the same time. Jonathan said that he sometimes gets sad because he feels that he had personally screwed up making a deal with The Wisconsin Group owner.

Immediately, Jonathan's demeanor became profoundly serious. Rather than looking at Suzanne, he started staring at me. Jonathan began to tell me the story about Noah and The Wisconsin Group! Noah is the president of The Wisconsin Group. During his and Noah's last phone call this past Friday, Jonathan told Noah that they hired a profit improvement consultant to come to Utah Off-road to grow the company's sales and make the business more profitable. Jonathan told Noah that Suzanne felt that if the consultant could make the company financially better, they could sell the business easier at a higher price. Jonathan said that Noah asked him what is the name of the consultant. Jonathan told him that it was Bob Curry. Jonathan told Noah that Bob Curry is the consultant who helped ABC Off-road Supply grow its sales and profits a year ago. Jonathan said, "Noah, I know the company owner, and since Bob Curry did his magic with that company, the owner, Brian, is a different man! Brian is the owner and general manager of ABC Off-road Supply. Before the consulting engagement, Brian was a stressful mess. One year after the consulting engagement ended, the company's sales have doubled, and the profits have skyrocketed. Brian and his partner are now paying themselves almost $1,000,000 in annual compensation from all the profits."

Noah asked Jonathan, "When is Bob Curry scheduled to come to Utah?" Jonathan answered, "This Monday was going to be his first day, and Bob said he would be here through Wednesday, flying home Thursday morning. Noah responded, "Jonathan, I know this guy! I just finished reading his three books. The title of the first book is From Red to Black, A Business Turnaround. After I read his first book, it was so good that I had to buy his other two books immediately. They are The Turnaround and The Turnaround 2. The Turnaround 2 is about your friend's company, ABC Off-road Supply. Jonathan, if you have not read his books, you should do so immediately.

There is so much quality business information in those three books. I could not believe it. Once you start reading each of Bob's books, you cannot set the book down until you have finished reading the last page. I have created a thorough list of his business-improving policies and procedures that he used in each book for the turnarounds. He refers to them as profit improvement recommendations or PIRs." I am using the information from Bob's books to develop a written business plan to introduce all his ideas that apply to our company's management team. Once I finish writing my goals, I will present the information to all our managers at our weekly executive management meeting. I aim to have our company grow in sales and profits like what Bob Curry did for your friend's business, ABC Off-road Supply." Noah said, "Jonathan, I would love to fly down to Utah and visit you this week to meet Bob Curry! Is that okay with you?"

Jonathan looked at me squarely and said, "Bob, Noah is flying to Utah to visit and meet you. Noah wants to hire you to consult with this group of companies." Jonathan then went on to tell me about all the different companies owned by The Wisconsin Group. The Wisconsin Group owns eight companies. I just sat there and listened to Jonathan as he talked. I started taking notes again, but this time, it was about Noah's company, not Utah Off-road. When Jonathan began to slow down telling the stories about this Wisconsin Group, I had my fourth cup of coffee. Suzanne was still sitting there watching Jonathan talk. Only now, since he was staring at me while he spoke, she remained silent during Jonathan's one-person conversation.

I lost track of time when our waiter came to our table and told us that the restaurant was closing at 11:00 a.m. He asked us if it would be okay if we moved into the lobby and talked there. We all looked at each other with slight embarrassment. We (Jonathan) had been talking for three hours and did not realize it. Suzanne then told the waiter that we would be leaving the restaurant immediately. I looked over my notes from our conversation. I had written down notes and comments for about 50% of my original list of questions. I learned valuable information at our three-hour breakfast meeting. I needed to know more about the topics I was interested in about Utah Off-road.

I had more notes about the company in Wisconsin than I did about my client in Utah. Jonathan was angry that Noah had strung him out for so long about buying his company. Then Jonathan told me another story about his conversations with Noah. Jonathan said, "Noah asked me about six months ago how much I wanted to sell Utah Off-road for. I told him $10,000,000.

Bob, Noah told me during an earlier conversation that his company bought another business and paid ten times EBITDA (EBITDA stands for Earnings Before Interest, Taxes, Depreciation, and Amortization) for the acquisition. Bob, if Noah paid ten times EBITDA for our company, Utah Off-road would be worth $10,000,000." *(See PIR #2 on page #45.)*

I had yet to see Jonathan and Suzanne's company's financial statements or the facility. I had no comment concerning the validity of the value of Jonathan and Suzanne's company. As intense as Jonathan was during this conversation, I knew this issue would arise again, especially if Noah traveled to Utah this week.

I signed the check for breakfast and charged all the meals to my hotel room. Then the three of us walked out together to the hotel parking lot. When we arrived at their Ford Bronco, I knew getting up in the passenger seat would be challenging. Jonathan had opened the door to his Ford Bronco for me to get into the front seat. Then he got in the back seat for our short commute to their manufacturing facility. I set my backpack on the floor of the vehicle and did my best to get in without looking like it was a huge struggle, which it was. Once I got into the front seat, I immediately put on my seat belt. Any ride in this offroad vehicle had the opportunity to be a real adventure.

Whatever happened to opening the truck's passenger door and quickly getting into the vehicle? It was a struggle for all three of us to get into the lifted Bronco. It is amusing that offroad enthusiasts spend substantial money on their vehicles to dress them up. After they finish the offroad upgrades, it is a significant struggle to even climb into the vehicle!

With Suzanne driving, it took us about 15 minutes to get to their company's manufacturing facility. While traveling to their company's location, I mentally recapped our conversations during breakfast. The truth was that I knew little about Jonathan's and Suzanne's company and the issues that were causing the business to be in trouble. I now believe that neither Jonathan nor his wife, Suzanne, knew the details about their problems and why the company was currently unsuccessful.

Profit Improvement Recommendations

PIR #1 – Dress for Success (Responsible Party – Jonathan and Suzanne)

Observation: The owner/president of a company should look and dress the part. Even in a manufacturing business, the leader/management team should wear a nice, clean, professional-looking pair of khakis and a dress shirt. Recruiting and hiring professional managers, sales staff, and employees won't be easy if the owner looks like a slob at work. If the owner dresses unprofessionally in his business environment, the management team will not respect him.

Conclusion: If you own a business, it is easy to show up at work every day looking like you care. The change in looking professional will make the people (managers, employees, customers, and vendors) think better about you and your business!

PIR Rating: I rate this PIR as a five out of ten. The owners dressing more professionally will change the overall attitude and morale of the company.

Action Plan: I plan to have a face-to-face meeting with the two owners of the business. They should improve their appearance so everyone (managers, employees, vendors, customers, bankers, and insurance agents) will immediately respect them. I don't want anyone to see them dressed like part of the staff working in the shop. (Completed on 8/9/22)

Financial Benefit: There is no logical way to estimate the actual economic benefit of this PIR. But for this PIR, I will use a conservative minimum of $20,000 for the next 12 months.

Deadline to Complete: August 31, 20XX

PIR #2 – Let the buyer make the first offer if you are selling your company. (Responsible Party – Jonathan)

Observation: When Jonathan told me the story about telling Noah that the sale price for his company was $10,000,000, I knew that he made a significant mistake. His mistake was that the seller should never be the first to quote a sale price for the business. The rule is: 'The first person who quotes a price loses!' When Noah asked Jonathan what price he would be willing to sell his company, Jonathan should have said to make him an offer.

Conclusion: In this case, Noah backed off from making an offer to buy the company because he knew that he and Jonathan were too far apart on the purchase price to agree. Jonathan's actions killed the deal, with no recent activity between Jonathan and Noah.

PIR Rating: I rate this PIR as a nine out of ten. Jonathan needs to gain experience in negotiating the sale price of his company. Jonathan's mistake killed the deal.

Action Plan: The action plan to help the owners of Utah Off-road sell their company is as follows:

1. The owners should hire an experienced business broker. The business broker will develop a formal appraisal of the value of the business. (Not necessary, decided not to sell)

2. Once an appraisal is complete and the owners agree on the company's evaluation, the business broker should market the business to potential buyers. (Not necessary, decided not to sell)

3. Jonathan and Suzanne should provide the broker with information about all the parties who expressed interest in purchasing their company recently. The broker can contact these people to determine if there is still interest in buying the business. (Not necessary, decided not to sell)

4. Once there are interested parties to purchase the company, the broker should negotiate with the potential buyer and keep Jonathan and Suzanne appraised of the status of the sale. (Not necessary, decided not to sell)

5. Then, when the brokor hao a purohase agreement signed by the buyer, and the owners agree on the terms and conditions of the sale, the broker should secure the seller's signatures. The broker should be responsible for managing all the exchange of information for the transaction up to and including the settlement between the two parties. This procedure may be the only way Jonathan and Suzanne can sell their business. (Not necessary, decided not to sell)

6. Later, during the consulting engagement, I discovered that the financial statements needed to be more accurate. The company needed a financial audit done before Utah Off-road could sell to a buyer. (Not necessary, decided not to sell)

Financial Benefit: This PIR is not easy to estimate the cost-benefit. I will use a conservative minimum of $200,000 for the next 12 months.

Deadline to Complete: December 31, 20XX

Chapter 3

THE PROBLEM WITH COMMON SENSE, IT IS NOT THAT COMMON.

"There are a handful of companies who understand all successful business operations come down to three basic principles: People—Product—Profit. Without top people, you cannot do much with the other two."
— *MALCOLM FORBES* – AN AMERICAN ENTREPRENEUR THE PUBLISHER OF FORBES MAGAZINE

Monday, August 7th – Day 1 of week 1
of the turnaround engagement

AFTER A SHORT 15-MINUTE DRIVE, WE ARRIVED at The Utah Off-road facility. The building was in a modern industrial park. Most of the buildings in this park looked like they were less than five years old. The industrial park was scenic, at least as industrial parks go. That was a big plus. If their facilities were old and run-down in an outdated industrial park, that would have presented additional problems, such as relocating the business.

Suzanne parked the Bronco by the front door. I opened the passenger door, unhooked my seat belt, and jumped out of the vehicle. In a normal Ford Bronco, one would open the passenger door, unhook the seat belt, put their right foot on the ground, and get up and out of the vehicle. With this Bronco lifted 15+ inches, the passenger opens the door and jumps out until they land on the ground.

The three of us walked in the front door together. Much to my surprise, the showroom looked like a junkyard. Five vehicles looked like work-in-progress in the large room, with each front and rear bumper removed and dismantled. Three other older vehicles were in the showroom, but I had no idea why. All the original bumper parts were lying on the floor around the perimeter of each car. Jonathan was modifying the Jeeps (Wrangler *and* a Gladiator), a Lexus SUV, and two Ford Broncos (Bronco Big Bend and Bronco Badlands) into offroad vehicles. Jonathan does this by removing the original stock bumpers and adding his newly designed bumpers with a big heavy winch on the front bumper and a spare tire rack on the back. After he mounts the bumpers and winches, he and Suzanne decide what else to add to the vehicles to *"bling"* them up. Whatever aftermarket parts that they decide on, Suzanne contacts other vendors to see if she can get the other offroad parts donated for the vehicles. She is usually successful and gets the parts donated. Vendors donate the parts because these vehicles will be displayed at the big *SEMA* show (*Specialty Equipment Market Association)* in Las Vegas in November. The SEMA show generates a high sales volume for offroad vendors after the show ends.

One of the Jeeps was black, and the Gladiator was gold. The Wrangler looked like an ordinary Jeep. The Gladiator looked like a Jeep pickup truck. Before that day, I had never seen a gold Jeep. The two Broncos were both brownish.

I humbly describe the colors of the vehicles because I am colorblind and have been since birth. I always check with my wife to get her approval about the colors I wear daily before leaving the house. I do not want to look stupid to my clients. The good news is that I can accurately identify the color of the white Lexus, the black and gold Jeeps, and the brownish Broncos, even with my handicap.

Unfortunately, Jonathan was slow to get these bumpers designed and installed! I had no clue why he would simultaneously work on five vehicles' front and rear bumpers. That's ten bumpers to design and install all at the same time, which is a very tall task for anyone. I said nothing, but my thoughts were: 'There is no excuse for their showroom to look this bad. These vehicles looked ridiculous, with all their bumpers and parts lying on the showroom floor. It leaves an inferior first impression on anyone who visits their facilities for the first time. The first time, second or third time.' Jonathan said, "Please excuse the mess, Bob. These are the vehicles that I am designing new aftermarket parts for. We will clean up this showroom within the next couple of months. These Jeeps, those Broncos, and Lexus are for the SEMA show in Las Vegas this November. I must focus and get them all done soon." I responded, "How long have these vehicles been in this showroom?" I asked the question because it looked like this showroom was in the same chaotic condition since they moved into this building five years ago. These cars had parts lying everywhere, and the room looked like an unmanaged, cluttered warehouse with junk all over the place. Jonathan answered my question defensively, "About six months." It was not a fatal issue with the facility looking as it is because cleaning it up is no big deal. A couple of laborers working during one weekend could do the job. It would take little time or payroll dollars to clean up the showroom, offices, and bathrooms and keep it that way in the future. When I started the last turnaround at ABC Off-road Supply, their shop/warehouse was in the same sloppy condition as this client's facility. They cleaned up the shop, warehouse, and showroom during one three-day weekend and did a beautiful job. I decided to put the messy conditions in the back of my mind and continue the tour, thinking about what changes I needed to make to this business to make it profitable.

I recently had a potential client in Fort Lauderdale in the swimming pool maintenance and construction industry. The two owners asked me to help them grow their sales and profits. My first meeting at their offices was my last meeting at their offices. The place was a dump. I asked them if they needed help finding and hiring qualified people for their company. Their answer was: *"YES, how did you know*?" I told both owners that no one wanted to work in an office resembling the city dump. The one younger owner said, "Bob, as long as the employees get their paychecks every week, what do they care about how the office looks?" My answer was, "Your employees can find a job anywhere. Many companies in the area are looking for good, qualified employees. They want to work for a company with a nice environment. They do not have to work in an office where they would be embarrassed to have a friend visit them at their employer's offices. After our conversation, I turned down the consulting engagement. Even though the potential client's office was in Fort Lauderdale,

I did not want to work in that dump that they called their office. After the owner's comment, I thought about the famous stand-up comedian Ron White. He told a funny story and then said, 'You can't fix stupid!' I only want to work with business owners who understand the condition of the company's office will impact their ability to hire highly qualified employees and make a profit. After doing turnaround consulting for over 25 years, I only accept turnaround engagements if the owners will listen to my direction. I do not accept engagements if the client struggles to make the necessary changes to their business to make it profitable. I shake their hand and wish those owners the absolute best. When I start with a client to fix their business, and the owner pulls the rope in the opposite direction, life is too short to deal with a client like that. I learned my lesson long ago; 'I cannot fix stupid!' (See PIR #3 on page #66.)

I looked at Jonathan with a very puzzled look on my face. Jonathan said, "Bob, you look confused. What's up?" I answered, "Jonathan, I am assuming that these cars in this showroom are all owned by your company, right?" Jonathan responded: "Yes, Bob, they are." I asked Jonathan: "If that is the case, I have a question for you. Why would you take money (five vehicles at an average of $60,000 each for a total of $300,000) out of the company's checking account to buy five vehicles when you could get the cars for free and earn a profit at the same time?" Now, it was Jonathan who had a puzzled look on his face. "Bob, I don't understand. How would I get these five vehicles for free?"

"Jonathan, you and I have a good friend, Brian, who owns a company about 10 miles south from here. He also deals in aftermarket offroad products (ABC Off-road Supply). His company does at least four times the sales volume that your company does. He has made deals with local dealerships in the Salt Lake City area. The dealerships deliver Jeeps, pickup trucks, and SUVs to Brian's shop. The auto mechanics in his shop install all the offroad products on those vehicles at a discounted labor rate per the dealership's purchase order. The dealerships love this deal because their vehicles sell faster with a higher profit margin when they have the aftermarket offroad parts installed. Brian now has an incredible increase in sales because he is selling to most of the local dealerships. These dealership customers deliver the vehicles to his business. His team in the shop upgrades the dealership's vehicles. The dealership's employees come to pick up the cars when Brian's team completes the installations. His mechanics work on the dealership vehicles when the shop's business is slow. The whole deal is extremely profitable for his company. His mechanics installed bumpers, lifts, wheels, tires, lights, camper tops, and hoists. Brian's company has not had to spend one dollar on dealership vehicles. But his company has deposited regular checks into his checking account for all the work done on those dealerships' vehicles."

I continued, "Jonathan, you should meet with the dealership's management and offer them a similar deal as Brian. That way, you could save your business a ton of money. You could design the new bumpers after the dealership delivers a vehicle to your facility. You would not have to worry about buying any more vehicles in the future. After you design and install your bumpers, you can take pictures of the vehicles and post them on your website and social media. You could also do the same for the other offroad products your company manufactures. You could do all this work and leave all the company's money in the checking account! So, the plan is to ask a dealership for one of their vehicles that you need to design the offroad bumpers. You could receive the vehicle at your shop, design the new bumper, install it, and have the dealership pick it up when your work is complete. When they pick up the vehicle, they will pay you for the new bumpers (front and back). You never need to spend any of the company's funds to buy any of the vehicles you need to design new offroad bumpers. You could also negotiate a deal with a dealership to bring their vehicle to *SEMA* to show without any out-of-pocket costs to your business. They would ask you to advertise their dealership on the vehicle at the show."

Jonathan stood there trying to figure out why the plan would not work. Jonathan is always terribly negative in our conversations. He puzzles me. Why hire a business consultant to improve your business's cash flow and profits, then argue against every suggestion he makes of the company? Rather than trying to figure out how to make something positive happen, he focuses on what could be wrong with the deal and why it would not work. He stood there for at least one minute thinking. It seemed like half an hour, and then finally said, "Bob, I think you are right; that may work!" I already knew it would work because my friend and client, Brian, made it work exceptionally well at his company. Unfortunately, everything is so negative with Jonathan before it becomes positive. I understand being conservative. I also understand much better being positive and creative to make a profit.

After Jonathan's and my conversation, I calculated the savings this PIR would save Jonathan's company. Those five vehicles cost the company at least $1,350 each per month for a total of $6,750 for the car loan payments. The auto insurance would cost another $1,000 per month for the five vehicles. If my numbers are close to right, the annual out-of-pocket cost would be over $93,000. Therefore, the business would save $93,000 and make a gross profit for every vehicle from each car dealership that it deals with in the future. (*See PIR #4 on page #68.*)

I wrote a note to add $250,000 to the sales budget when Jonathan visits the local dealerships to sell his company's offroad products. The estimated profit improvement for these two recommendations should be $94,000. I also noted the cost of hiring a professional cleaning firm to visit the company weekly to keep the facility clean and professional, especially the company's showroom, offices, and bathrooms.

Later that day, Jonathan's truly negative personality surfaced again. He said, "Bob, something was bugging me about your suggested deal concerning not buying the cars when the car manufacturers release the new models. I buy these cars because of the big tax benefit with the transaction." I responded, "Jonathan, how does that work?" "Bob, if we are having a great profitable year, the company will pay a big federal income bill. By buying these vehicles, the purchase has given us a great tax benefit. Last year, we expensed these vehicles rather than adding them to the fixed assets on our company's balance sheet and depreciating them over three to four years?" I asked, "Are you telling me that you purchased $300,000 of vehicles for your company to use in the business and expensed the whole $300,000? How much money did you spend on the purchase when you financed the Jeeps, Lexus, and Broncos?"

"The bank wanted $40,000 down, and we financed the balance of $260,000 over four years." "You took a tax deduction of $300,000 even though you only put $40,000 down on the deal?" Jonathan looked at me as his face turned red and said, "Yeah, that is right." "Jonathan, I have a master's degree from Widener University in taxation. It would be best if you did not take my comments as the gospel about the current tax law because I graduated in the 1980s. The tax law changes yearly. I do not spend time staying current with tax law amendments. There is no way the IRS will let you expense $300,000 of vehicles all in the first year that you purchased them so you can reduce your tax liability for the current year, especially when you only put $40,000 down on the purchase of the vehicles. Jonathan, you need to talk to your tax accountant and make him aware of the details of that transaction. Did you talk to him about this transaction before filing your current year's tax return?" "No, Bob, I didn't; I was too busy then!" *(See PIR #5 on page #70.)*

Parked by the front door in the showroom was a white Lexus SUV. It looked like the car's front bumper was in an accident, and all the broken parts were lying on the floor. The Lexus' body was filthy. I later learned that they took the vehicle offroad in the mud at Moab, Utah. I just kept quiet because I was thinking about what other significant problems would pop up. We had been in the building briefly, and it started poorly. Suzanne and I followed Jonathan, who led me through the showroom. He was explaining the status of each disassembled vehicle. During the first part of this tour, I thought if this were my company, I would be embarrassed. I was touring my client's facilities, and it was awful. It was hard for me to believe that anyone would let their business look this bad, but it was right there in front of my eyes.

I asked Suzanne where I should set down my backpack with my laptop computer before we continued the tour of the manufacturing shop area. She told me to follow her to her office, and I could put my stuff down there. I hate to say this, but her office was in the same condition as the showroom. Her large office had piles of junk everywhere. Her desk was in the middle of the room, and a large conference table was between her desk and the office door. I could tell when we walked in she saw the look on my face, and she was embarrassed. The only open spot in her office to set down my backpack was on the conference room table. Jonathan waited for us to return from Suzanne's office, and then we continued our tour.

I followed Jonathan to the shop. When we arrived, my first impression was that it was noticeably quiet for a manufacturing plant fabricating mostly heavy steel offroad bumpers. The low noise level was because only a few employees worked in this 15,000 sq. ft. shop. The shop area was quiet when few or no power tools were cutting, bending, welding, or grinding thick metal for offroad bumpers. Normally, we would need earplugs to protect our ears from the loud noise from all the bumper fabrication. Usually, in a fabrication shop, cutters, grinders, and welders are very loud. I was wrong, and in the next 20 minutes, I was about to find out why this area was so quiet.

A huge machine was on the other side of the door leading from the showroom. Jonathan said that this machine, "The Bender," is only six months old, and he had bought it at last year's *SEMA* show. Jonathan noted that the equipment vendor had the machine displayed at the show. After the show, Jonathan learned that the company would ship the giant device back to their facility in Sweden.

Jonathan offered the company owner a deal. He would buy the device if the owner gave him a deep discount on the retail sales price of the machine. With his deal, the company must deliver the machine to their facility in Utah and set it up to operate correctly. The machine owner gave Jonathan an excellent discount on the sale price. The owner also sent one of their technicians to Jonathan's facility to install the machine and train the staff to operate it properly. Jonathan was proud of the deal he made to buy the bender and have it installed.

A high school-age young man sat beside the machine playing a video game on his phone. Jonathan grabbed him by the arm and told Bill, his son, to put the game away.

Jonathan wanted to introduce Bill to the new "Manufacturing Efficiency Expert" he had just hired. Suzanne and Jonathan created a new title for me to keep the whole company and their family from knowing they had just hired a Turnaround Specialist. My actual title did not work politically well for the image they wanted to convey to all the workers. I reached out to shake Bill's hand. I introduced myself as Bob Curry and told him I was glad to meet him. Bill was timid and seemed surprised to shake anyone's hand in the shop.

Two machine technicians were atop the bender machine, trying to fix something. I asked Bill, what were those two guys doing to the device? Jonathan answered my question instead of Bill. He said, "Bob, my son started the machine yesterday morning with the pipe loaded wrong. It broke two very delicate components on the machine. These two guys are from a local dealer for this machine. They are here to replace the broken parts to keep the machine running. Unfortunately, Bill thought playing his video game was okay while running this $600,000 machine. As it turns out, he was wrong." I looked at Bill; his head was down, and he slowly slipped his cell phone into his back pocket. Jonathan said for Bill's benefit, "These two guys cost the company $4,000 the minute that they walked through our front door, and that does not include the cost of the broken parts that they will have to replace to get the machine running again." Bill returned to the chair he was sitting in when we walked into the shop and sat down. I could tell that Jonathan's son felt terrible and embarrassed because his father yelled at him with me present. *(See PIR #6 on page #72.)*

Jonathan explained to me what the machine does when it works correctly and how it has saved hundreds of person-hours when running properly.

Jonathan then explained that seven employees, not including his son, are currently working in the shop area. One guy (George) is cutting the metal sheets, four employees are doing the first welding, one is in shipping, and one is in the inventory racks. He is repacking the parts used to install the bumpers. He was getting the packages ready to ship with each bumper. That employee is also responsible for taking the bumpers across the street in the industrial park to have them powder coated.

I said, "Jonathan, other than the broken bending machine, do you have any other problems with the equipment in this shop?" Jonathan looked at me as I asked my question and said, "Bob, follow me. I will give you a *'50-cent tour'* of the whole shop. And yes, we have other operating problems here in the shop." Jonathan walked over to the cutter machine and introduced me to George, the operator. I shook George's hand and introduced myself. George said, "Bob, I know who you are; you have authored three books about business. I am friends with the good people who work at ABC Off-road Supply. I heard about what a wonderful job you did for them and how profitable the company is now. I prayed you would come to our company next and do the same for us. Bob, since today is only your first day here, I will reserve my comments so you can draw your conclusions." George lowered his voice, moved closer to me, and whispered, "Bob, we need help!" Jonathan said, "George, if you don't have anything positive to say, would you please tell Bob about the machine you are running?" George gave Jonathan a smart-alecky look. He then returned to me and gave a detailed operating review of the cutter. When he finished, George asked me, "Bob, if I bring in my copies of your books, would you please autograph them for me?" I answered, "George, I will, my friend!"

Jonathan said, "Please, sir, follow me; I want you to see our robotic welders and grinders next." We walked about 25 feet down the aisle from the cutter to the four robotic machines. They were both sitting there idle. Surprisingly, Jonathan was smiling because he was so proud of these four machines, the two robotic welders and the two robotic grinders. The grinders were 25 feet further down the aisle. Jonathan was standing next to the two robotic welders, and I noticed dust all over both machines. I asked him why the machines were so dusty. He answered, "When these two machines operate properly, they will weld a bumper four times faster than a human can weld one."

I said, "That is impressive, but why are they all dusty and not being used right now?" After a long hesitation before answering my question, he said, "These machines require a great deal of computer programming to operate properly. When I bought them, the vendor sent in a programmer who was young and dumb! He worked on both the welders and grinders and could not get either of them operating. The salesperson from the company told me to go out and find a third-party programmer, and they would reimburse me for the cost." I said, "So I am guessing that finding a qualified programmer to get these bad boys operating is not that easy." Suzanne said, "Bob, we have an employee attending college locally to become a certified welder. As part of the curriculum, for him to get his welding certification, he must take classes on programming these types of robots. Unfortunately, he has been sick for three months and dropped out of college this semester." I asked the two owners, "So, how long ago did you purchase these pieces of equipment?" Jonathan answered, "Seven months ago, at the end of this month. Bob, I have not made any installment payments for any of these robots, and I will not until we get them operating." "So, my good friend, what is your plan to get these machines operating?" "Bob, Suzanne just put an ad in the local newspaper and on *Indeed,* the internet company, to find a qualified programmer to program these machines." I asked the obvious question for Jonathan or Suzanne to answer: "Have you talked any more to the vendor? I am sure that they are interested in getting these machines running since they want paid for these four machines!" I could see that Jonathan was upset about our conversation concerning his idle robots. He said, "Bob, the salesperson that sold me the machines and his boss no longer work for that company. The company is in such disarray; they might not even know I have not paid them the last seven installments." The only thing I could think of was, 'WOW, WHAT A MESS!'

I decided to share with these two owners how a turnaround consultant thinks about this situation. I said, "Jonathan and Suzanne, as you can imagine, I have been a businessperson for a long time. I evaluate business situations by calculating the budgetary and cash flow impact on the company for every decision I make when I run a company or turn one around. For example, let us first discuss your four robotic machines. I do not know what you paid for them, but before I had purchased the machines, I would have calculated my Return On Investment or "ROI" during normal operations. When these machines are operating properly, your ROI is very profitable. According to what you said earlier, robots can weld a bumper four times faster than humans. That caught my attention. You are paying your welders an average of $20 per hour, and with taxes and benefits, they each cost you about $26 per hour. The robots can do four times the work or replace three employees on your shop floor when this robot is working properly. You would have to have one employee 100% dedicated to overseeing the production of the two machines. Therefore, the robots are doing the work of seven employees in one hour, lowering your labor cost by seven times $26 or $182 per hour. That calculates reducing your cost of goods by $1,456 per day or $7,280 per week. The welding robots would have my attention if I owned this company. If your grinding robots have the same cost benefit as the welding robots, they will reduce the cost of goods for your bumpers by $14,560 per week or $728,000 annually. Jonathan, by you not paying attention to getting these robotic machines operating properly, you are losing $728,000 that would drop directly to your bottom line." *(See PIR #7 on page #73.)*

I continued, "The budgetary impact is much larger than that. Because you have a 26-week order backlog, I know you are losing orders to your competitors. Suppose your competitors can ship their customer orders in two to three weeks. In that case, your competitors will get 90% to 95% of the offroad bumper orders, especially when your customer order person says, "Thank you for your order on March 1st. We will ship your bumper to you in the first week of October, six months later than when that customer placed the order. Does that make any sense to you?"

Suzanne looked at me with a stern look on her face and said, "Mr. Curry, I need to speak up here. You are being too hard on Jonathan. He is trying his best to make this company profitable and has a massive amount of stress on his shoulders. You should know that he does not need additional pressure from you!" "Hmm…Suzanne, I am not trying to put additional stress on anyone's shoulders! It's just the opposite. Let me ask you a question – How would the company's financial statements and bank account look if we added $728,000 to the profits and cash balance? And may I add, this is only one issue. I plan to develop a comprehensive business plan to make several changes to your operations that will make your company very profitable. I am going to let you in on a business secret! Making a big profit from your business is much less stressful than losing money. Making a large profit reduces the stress on your company's cash position. If you do not believe me, please call Brian at ABC Off-road Supply and ask him that question!"

Jonathan and I walked around the shop for my tour. I noticed many unfinished bumpers on storage racks, with the racks parked anywhere and everywhere around the shop. All the bumpers were at various stages of work-in-process fabrication. Before I asked Jonathan about all the bumpers on the racks, I tried to figure out the answer myself before I popped the question to Jonathan. "Jonathan, I have a question. Storing these bumpers on these racks everywhere in the shop, what is that all about?" Jonathan answered, "Bob, those bumpers are our customer orders at various stages of fabrication. We need more employees to staff each fabricating station (bending, cutting, welding 1, grinding, welding 2, powder coating, and shipping). Until we can find more welders, we must build the bumpers in stages. Typically, one of the welders is working on the bending machine when my son is not watching the machine. George is the only employee who can operate the cutter efficiently, so he runs that machine full-time. Our four welders will do the first welding process on the bumpers for one week, and then those four guys will move over to work on the grinding needed on the existing work-in-process inventory. After grinding as many bumpers as possible, they move over to do the welding 2 processes. Those bumpers (Jonathan pointed at a bunch of racks of bumpers) are through the welding 2 processes and have a thorough quality control inspection. After the inspection, we load the bumpers on a cart and transport them across the driveway to our powder coating vendor by the employee who oversees our shipping.

Our powder coating vendor has had substandard quality control problems with their work. Immediately after we bring a rack of bumpers back from the vendor, we do a detailed inspection of each bumper. We need to find a new powder coating vendor because the one we have now is costing us money. Sometimes, it takes them one week to ten days to send us back ten perfect powder coated bumpers without a problem. In the worst case, if the powder coating vendor has a quality operation, we should get the bumpers back in one to two days. Unfortunately, we have more orders than we can stay current with our manufacturing processes. As of today, we have approximately six months of backorders for our bumpers and other offroad products that we sell." Jonathan said that the backorders continue to grow because we need the staff or the robots to stay current with the customer orders. I considered interrupting Jonathan when he said the company had six months of back orders, which was getting worse, but I didn't. I had many questions to ask Jonathan about the shop's status. Still, I decided to hold my questions until I had more time to sit down and make a comprehensive list of all the issues I observed about the shop operations.

As the three of us walked over to the warehousing area of the shop, I decided that I did not want to wait to hear the story about the six months of backlog orders. The more I heard about Utah Off-road, the better I could put together my turnaround plan. I asked, "Jonathan, please tell me more about the six months of the backlog of manufacturing bumpers to fulfill your customer orders. I can understand having four to six weeks of orders on your backlog list; I cannot understand six months." "Bob, there is an easy answer to your question! We cannot manufacture the bumpers as fast as we get the customer orders." "Jonathan, that is clear to me. My question is, why?"

"Bob, we cannot hire shop talent (certified welders) to manufacture the bumpers quickly enough. The demand for aftermarket offroad products is stronger than our ability to manufacture the products. Good welders are hard to find at the salary we pay our group in the shop. We pay our welders about $17 to $20 per hour. Zero candidates with a welding certification in this area will accept $17 per hour." At this point, I knew what the problem was. "Bob, the going hourly rate for welders on the street right now is $24 to $27 per hour, which is $7 to $10 higher than we are currently paying." Immediately, I thought that this was one of those classic cases where – 'The problem with common sense, it is not that common' applies. After a few minutes, I decided the two owners caused this issue by not having enough business training or education before starting this company. Because I knew that Jonathan and Suzanne were knowledgeable people, Ron White's famous quote: 'You cannot fix stupid!' did not apply.

I knew if I started to explain to Jonathan that he needed to hire more welders to fabricate the backlog of bumper orders, even at a premium hourly wage for welders, he would argue with me that the company could not afford any more cost on the labor force. Having a six-month backlog of customer orders for offroad bumpers was a material problem for this business. This backlog problem causes many issues, such as:

1. Their customers will not wait for a discretionary spending type of purchase for six months. Shipping a customer's order needs to be two to three weeks.

2. If the company did what was necessary to improve its production and reduce the backlog of orders, its sales would increase due to the demand for the products.

Profit Improvement Recommendations

PIR #3 – Keep the shop, showroom, offices, parking lot, vehicles, and bathrooms clean and looking professional. (Responsible Party – Jonathan and Suzanne)

Observation: The mess in the showroom looked like it had been in this condition for a long time. The cluttered showroom sends a poor message to customers, vendors, bankers, insurance brokers, employees, and one turnaround consultant who walks through the front door into this showroom. It visually says that it is okay for the owners, managers, and employees to not respect their workplace at this company, including the showroom.

The first appearance creates a financially distressed image for the company. The company is ready to file for bankruptcy protection and shut down the business soon. Unfortunately, the status of the rest of the company was in the same condition as the showroom, which included the company's offices, manufacturing shop, and bathrooms.

Conclusion: The company's overall appearance is essential to make a good impression on visitors when the owners try recruiting and hiring top-quality employees.

Secondly, and equally important, if the owners try to sell the company at its maximum sales price, they will be unable to do it if the showroom looks like a garbage dump. When the owners coordinate the company's cleaning, it will send a clear message to all the existing employees to treat the business as if they are working for a first-class organization.

PIR Rating: I rate this problem as six out of ten.

Action Plan: The action plan to clean up the Utah Off-road facility will start immediately.

1. The owners should hire a cleaning service to clean the showroom, offices, and bathrooms once a week. (Completed on 8/19/20XX)

2. All company-owned vehicles will be the responsibility of the person driving the car to keep it clean. There should be a formal inspection of each vehicle weekly. (Completed on 8/19/20XX)

3. Every worker in the shop will be responsible for cleaning their own designed area before Monday, giving everyone seven days to clean the shop and then keep it clean. (Completed on 8/19/20XX)

4. The shop staff will move all the work-in-process inventory from the aisles in the shop to one designed area convenient to each fabrication station, improving the safety conditions. (Completed on 8/19/20XX)

Financial Benefit: This PIR is not easy to estimate the cost-benefit, so I will use a conservative minimum of $20,000 for the next 12 months.

Deadline to Complete: August 31, 20XX

PIR #4 – Thinking out of the box to improve the cash flow of your business. (Responsible Party – Jonathan)

Observation: Jonathan, unlike Brian, the owner of ABC Off-road Supply, needed help to think out of the box for his business to be more profitable. Brian grew his company's sales and profits by selling offroad products to local dealerships in the Salt Lake City area. The dealership sales for Brian's company materially improved the cash flow for ABC Off-road Supply.

Conclusion: Jonathan, on the other hand, purchased five vehicles from local dealerships and used the cars to design his new bumpers. The out-of-pocket costs for Jonathan's company were substantial for the cars parked in the showroom. If Jonathan was an out-of-the-box thinker like Brian, his company could have eliminated the expenses of buying the five vehicles and grown the sales by selling his offroad products to the local dealerships.

PIR Rating: I rate this PIR as an eight out of ten. Jonathan's inability and lack of business savvy, training, and education caused his company to spend considerable money needlessly. He could have had the vehicles for free to design the offroad bumpers for the new models released by the car manufacturers.

Action Plan: My plan to help Jonathan with this costly transaction, I would suggest that:

1. Jonathan immediately starts working on and completing the designs for the new bumpers for the five vehicles parked in the company's showroom. (Completed on 8/19/20XX)

2. Once the vehicles are in resale condition, the person responsible for the marketing and the company's website should have the vehicles detailed and pictures taken of the new bumpers. The employee will post the pictures on the internet and the company's website. (Completed on 8/19/20XX)

3. In the future, when a car manufacturer releases a new vehicle that would be a suitable candidate for aftermarket offroad bumper sales, Jonathan should call on the local dealerships for that vehicle if they would like a brand new offroad bumper designed and installed at a discounted price. Once Jonathan makes a deal with the dealership, he should prioritize his time to design and install the products for that vehicle. With this procedure, the company would never be out-of-pocket for creating a new product. (Completed on 8/19/20XX)

Financial Benefit: When Jonathan uses the above method of getting new manufacturer vehicles for models to design the offroad products, the company will reduce its costs annually by $93,000. Utah Off-road would gain $250,000 in retail sales during the first year of this new process.

Deadline to Complete: December 31, 20XX

PIR #5 – Seek tax advice from your tax expert. (Responsible Party – Suzanne)

Observation: Even though this was my first day onsite at Utah Off-road, I could see serious issues with this company becoming truly profitable again. After the conversation with Jonathan about expensing five vehicles in the current year rather than booking them as fixed assets and depreciating them over three or four years, I knew that I would have big problems once I started reviewing the financial side of this business.

Conclusion: Jonathan was proud of himself that he bought these five vehicles with a $40,000 down payment and a loan for the balance of $260,000. He believed he could write off 100% of the cars against the current year's income, therefore, he would not have to pay any corporate income taxes.

Unfortunately, his handling of the transaction in that manner was not legal. If the IRS audited the company, there would be some significant adjustments to the company's income and tax liability, including additional penalties and interest.

PIR Rating: I rate this problem as ten out of ten. Jonathan's lack of knowledge and experience with accounting, taxes, and financial statements puts the company at risk.

Action Plan: My plan to help Utah Off-road is to schedule a meeting with the tax preparer who did the current tax return and discuss the matter with him in detail.

1. Because the two owners are so naïve about many areas of business, especially finance and taxes, they should immediately search for a qualified candidate to hire as the company's controller to manage the financial department. The controller should be responsible for cleaning up the tax return mess and keeping the financial statements current and accurate. (Completed on 12/31/20XX)

2. Once the company's financial statements are current, the controller should hire a CPA firm to audit the balance sheet, income statement, and company tax returns for the past three years and amend the returns where necessary. (Completed on 10/31/20XX)

Financial Benefit: Utah Off-road is at risk with the Internal Revenue Service for taking illegal deductions on its corporate tax returns. This mistake would generate penalties, interest charges, additional tax preparation fees, and possible legal costs because they may need a lawyer to defend their tax position.

This PIR is not easy to estimate the cost-benefit, so I will use a conservative minimum of $20,000 for the next 12 months.

Deadline to Complete: December 31, 20XX

PIR #6 – Seventeen-year-old son and video games do not belong in a fabrication shop. (Responsible Party – Jonathan and Suzanne)

Observation: For Jonathan to put his unsupervised 17-year-old high schooler in charge of running a $600,000 machine in the fabrication shop was at the pinnacle of bad decisions. First, the son must be older and more mature to understand the danger of such equipment. Second, while his son needed to manage the machine, he played video games on his phone.

Conclusion: - Jonathan's unwise decision cost him:

1. The company would have to pay $5,000 for the damages to one of the shop's essential production machines.

2. There would be production downtime due to the damage done to the machine.

3. I am sure every shop employee has witnessed the owner's son playing video games on his phone during work hours, creating a terrible image for a shop employee.

4. A high school student is not mature enough at 17 to run a $600,000 piece of equipment in a manufacturing environment.

PIR Rating: I rate this problem a ten out of a possible ten. The list above suggests that fixing this issue is important concerning the young man's safety.

Action Plan: My plan to resolve these problems:

1. The 17-year-old son of Jonathan and Suzanne is too young to be in a shop building offroad bumpers using heavy metal. If the owners want their son to work in the business, he should work in customer service, accounting, or marketing. (Completed on 8/7/20XX)

2. Shop employees may not use cell phones in the shop area. (Completed on 8/7/20XX)

Financial Benefit: Even though the business owners may have several reasons to give their teenage son a job to teach him the value of a dollar when earned, the job should not be in the shop where he could easily hurt himself or other people in the shop. A position in the customer service, advertising, or accounting departments is better suited for a high schooler. The bender is an expensive and vital piece of equipment in the company's fabrication process. When the machine is down due to damage or repairs, it stops the production of offroad bumpers. Having a qualified operator overseeing the operation of the machine will save the company $50,000.

Deadline to Complete: August 7, 20XX

PIR #7 – Four robotic machines are not operating in the shop. (Responsible Party – Jonathan)

Observation: For Jonathan to have four robotic pieces of equipment sitting on his shop floor, not operating for over six months, is ridiculous. He should have done due diligence for the company and the equipment before he agreed to buy them and put the machines in his shop.

Conclusion: If the programming skills to make this equipment operate are so rare, they should return the equipment to the manufacturer and look for other companies to purchase different equipment to use.

PIR Rating: I rate this problem as a ten out of ten because of the reduction of labor costs when these machines are operating correctly.

Action Plan: My plan to resolve these problems:

1. Jonathan should first research the manufacturing company he purchased the robots from to determine if he should keep the machines or return them to the manufacturer. (Completed on 8/19/20XX)

2. Jonathan should contact the company to have their computer technicians visit Utah Off-road to program the robotic welders and grinders. This problem should have gone away when Jonathan bought the machines months ago. (Completed on 8/22/20XX)

3. Jonathan should have demanded that the manufacturer of the robots find a new programmer rather than his company have the responsibility. (Did not follow this action plan)

4. Utah Off-road should hire an employee skilled in programming. A second option is to have one of the company's employees sent to school at WSU to program the robots,

so these machines always operate efficiently. (Completed on 8/19/20XX)

Financial Benefit: The added cost that the company is experiencing is approximately $728,000 annually, which does not include the lost revenue from having the 26-week customer order backlog.

Deadline to Complete: August 31, 20XX

Chapter 4

TWENTY-SIX WEEKS BACKLOG

*"Step out of the history that is holding you back.
Step into the new story you are willing to create."*

*— OPRAH WINFREY – TALK SHOW HOST,
PRODUCER, ACTRESS, AUTHOR
AND PHILANTHROPHIST*

Monday, August 8th – Day 1 of week 1
of the turnaround engagement

WE FINISHED THE SHOWROOM TOUR AND THE demo of the machines in the shop. The machines: one bender, one cutter, two welders, and two grinders were expensive. Then, Jonathan told me about all the problems with their powder coating firm. The Utah Off-road has been using this firm to powder coat their bumpers once they were through all the fabrication processes. Utah Off-road has used this company for only six months. The company was right across the street from their facility in the same industrial park, making the powder coater very convenient.

Jonathan told me that his employee in the shipping department, Jake, would deliver and pick up a rack of bumpers at the powder coating company. Upon a thorough inspection, Jake would find at least one bumper in five had problems when he returned to the shop with the bumpers. Jake returned the problem bumpers to the powder coating vendor because of the quality issues with the finished product. There were runs in the paint, which was unexpected by Jonathan and, more importantly, the customers. They also had problems with different shades of the paint color on the same bumper.

I asked Jonathan why our employee did not inspect the powder coating quality at the vendor's location, so it was unnecessary to transport the bad ones back to the powder coating company. He just looked at me like he did not have a conclusive answer to my question. I could see Suzanne, out of the corner of my eye, pull out a small notepad and write down a reminder about my suggestion.

I said, "Jonathan, a 20% error factor on the powder coating process is bad. Is there anything that you can do with the vendor to improve their powder coating quality?" Jonathan said, "I know the owner of the company. He is an old friend of mine. That is 50% of why we use his company for powder coating. As you can imagine, the other 50% is because his company is right across the street from our facility. The owner used to live locally here in Utah but recently moved to Phoenix, Arizona. He is getting ready to retire and sell his company. If he knew that the powder coating process in his company was this bad, his head would explode. There would also be heads rolling across the street. He is a former drill sergeant in the army. He served in the Vietnam War. Being a drill sergeant is still a big part of his personality!" I asked, "When did you last meet with this old sergeant?" Jonathan explained, "I met with him for three hours talking about the operational process and pricing between our two companies when we first started using his company. Immediately after our meeting, he relocated to Phoenix."

I wondered why Jonathan would not give him a call to alert the owner of the inferior quality of his company's powder coating operation. When the drill sergeant became an absentee owner of his powder coating company, their customer service decreased. Jonathan's look got serious, and he explained, "Mr. Curry, as you have noticed, as you are touring our shop, we have approximately 26 weeks of customer orders on our backlog report. I understand that 26 weeks is a considerable backlog, but the powder coating operation is not causing a big delay in shipping our orders to the customers! There is still a strong demand for our products, or we will not have a huge backlog problem.

If I called the owner to complain about the quality of their powder coating, he would come up here and kick some butt in their operations department!" I asked, "And the problem with that is what?" This situation is another one of those conversations with Jonathan; I do not understand his logic. "Help me understand: Would it not be better for your company if their powder coating operation was much better quality? Wouldn't it be better for the business if you did not have to return 20% of the bumpers?" "Yes, Bob, of course, you are right. I do not want their management or employees thinking that I am tattle-tailing on them about the inferior quality of their powder coating to their owner all the time." I asked, "Are you satisfied with the quality of their powder coating, and if not, what will you do about it? Their problems are costing your company a lot of money! You do understand that, right?"

If we make all these positive changes in the shop, we will produce at least three times the number of bumpers compared to the existing production rate. If we start delivering three times the number of bumpers to our powder coating firm, they will not be able to stay up with our volume. There is a problem with their shop with today's volume of work that we are delivering to their shop. If our production doubles or triples, the powder coating operation will quickly become a huge problem.

I asked Jonathan, "Can you think of a plan to resolve our current problem with your powder coating company and, more importantly, our potential future problem? We must deal with this issue now rather than wait and have a three times bigger production problem." Jonathan said, "I talked to a friend of mine in the area that does a great deal of powder coating, which includes some of the companies in this industrial park. I am in the process of setting up a meeting with them. Last night, I called the owner of the company that we currently use and shared with him about our struggles with his company. He promised to schedule a trip here to deal with the problems because he does not want to lose our account. Brian and I are having lunch together this weekend. He will give me some ideas and contacts on how I can fix our potential powder coating problems." *(See PIR #8 on page #87.)*

Jonathan looked frustrated and said, "I have a whole list of bigger problems I must deal with first. I need to get all our robots programmed and operating properly. I need to hire a good shop supervisor to manage all the employees working in the shop. I need to find and hire cheaper labor (welders) for our shop. I need to get my 26-week backlog of orders down to a reasonable number. I need to get bumpers and other offroad equipment designed and installed for those five vehicles in the showroom. I need to rewrite the installation instructions for about 90% of the equipment that we sell. And I need to add this problem to my list! I need to speak to the owner of the powder coating company again to fix their quality problems, or we will move to a new powder coating vendor."

Jonathan did not know how to handle the stress of everything happening in the shop. He knew he did not have the time or talent to run this company. I looked at Suzanne, and she had the very same look on her face.

I asked Jonathan, "Do you know how to eat an elephant?" He looked at me like I was being ridiculous! "I will share a secret about the turnaround consulting business I have been doing for the past 25 years! I have consulted with large companies with over a billion dollars in sales and smaller companies like Utah Off-road. It will surprise you, but I find many problems common in larger and smaller companies. Here is what I just heard from you. You know all the problems within your company but do not know how to fix them organizationally."

"I am guessing that you go home every night overwhelmed and worrying the whole evening about what to do and how to fix your company's problems. Jonathan, how about the three of us return to Suzanne's conference table in her office and discuss all the problems and how we fix them?" Suzanne asked, "Okay, Bob, how do you eat an elephant?" I smiled at her and said, "One bite at a time! We will document all the operating issues with this company and develop a plan to solve them one problem at a time. The company's profitability and cash flow will improve with each situation we resolve. Today is only my first day here. I have uncovered several problems, which we will fix. My normal process is to develop a written plan on how we will attack all the issues in an organized manner. Once I create the turnaround plan, we will prioritize it. I first resolve the problems that have the biggest budgetary impact on the company. Then, we deal with the second largest simultaneously or immediately after fixing the first problem. I keep attacking and solving the issues. Solving these issues makes the company profitable."

Suzanne spoke up and asked, "Bob, where have you been for the past five years? We needed your business wisdom and guidance when we started this company. Jonathan's father and brother have attempted to share their wisdom and guidance with Jonathan, and we have been so close to a crash-and-burn status so many times that I cannot count them. I wish they had left Jonathan alone and let him learn how to manage this company to profitability. Jonathan is very smart, but when he gets frustrated with his family, his mind shuts down, and all his productivity stops. We are currently at one of those points and have been for the past six months. Jonathan has not slept well in half a year because he worries about this place and our family if the business goes down. The less sleep he gets, the higher his frustration level is." Jonathan stopped Suzanne mid-sentence and said, "Can we continue this conversation in the privacy of your office rather than out here in the shop where all our employees can hear this conversation?"

As the three of us were walking to Suzanne's office, I had many things bouncing around in my brain about Jonathan and Utah Off-road. When we arrived at Suzanne's office, I asked the two owners if I could have an hour to write down everything that I learned today and get it organized. The hour would also give Jonathan time to settle down and destress. They both smiled and agreed, then left the office.

I knew that I had yet to see the company's financial statements. I was mentally prepared to review the worst financial statements in my turnaround consulting career. The financial statements were not my focus yet. Usually, financial reporting is one of the first things I review during a consulting engagement, but something else is needed here. My biggest problem right now was understanding the 26 weeks of customers' orders needing to be fabricated and shipped to the customers. My goal was to fix those issues as soon as possible.

I had run into this same problem with a hurricane shutter company in Florida that I turned around several years ago. I documented the problem and its resolution in my first book, From Red to Black, A Business Turnaround. I solved the problem by removing the manager who was responsible for but not supervising the installation staff. That supervisor was also stealing inventory from the business. Most installers who reported to this supervisor were at a bar daily, drinking their lunch from 11:00 a.m. until 2:00 p.m. rather than installing hurricane shutters. Solving this problem helped the company's sales and profits to double during the next 12 months.

I learned a long time ago that a company with unsupervised employees working in the field needs to have alternative ways to supervise those employees. There are several ways to manage employees in the field, and we used various methods.

1. We installed GPS systems in each of their company vans. We could then track exactly where every installation vehicle was from when they left the company's parking lot until they returned each evening. We were sure to make every installation team aware that we knew exactly where their van was every minute of every day.

2. The operational reporting system gave the owner and all management current and accurate information. By

doing this, they knew exactly how each hurricane shutter installation job was progressing. We reported the weekly installation results on the company's conference room whiteboard. The reporting enabled everyone to see the average number of hurricane shutters installed per installation team weekly. Peer pressure between all the installation teams was a strong tool to motivate each team to improve their production.

3. We hired two new installation supervisors to ride around daily to each installation site for a daily inspection of their progress with their installation jobs.

4. We upgraded the talent of our installation teams by hiring better-qualified technicians to install the hurricane shutters.

5. We created an incentive plan to reward each installation team if they accomplished their goal of finishing each customer job within the budgeted allotment of time or quicker. The incentive plan also included a quality control inspection by the installation supervisor for the team to earn their bonus at the end of each job. The incentive rewards were a substantial part of their compensation. If an installation team does not receive approval for their bonus for a job, it is painful for their monthly paycheck.

Utah Off-road had a much easier problem to resolve to improve the production of their offroad products. All their employees were right in the shop, only steps away from the two owners. They were all easy to supervise. At this point of the consulting engagement, I needed to learn how efficient the shop employees were at their jobs (bending, cutting, welding

1, grinding, welding 2, powder coating, and shipping). The cause of this problem was no operational reporting and the understaffing of the shop operations.

At this time, I was feeling sad about Jonathan and Suzanne. They have built a nice company with quality offroad products in high demand with their customers. The problem is that the company grew larger than they could manage properly. This situation is common in my consulting practice. A business outgrowing the skills and abilities of the owners is a frequent problem. My job with this engagement is to clean up this mess and sell the business to a new owner with the leadership skills and ability to manage this company as it grows and keeps it profitable.

One thing that concerned me was about what Jonathan said earlier. He commented, "I need to find and hire cheaper labor (welders) for our shop. We pay our welders an average of $20 per hour. Now, the kids who graduate from the technical colleges in the area who come here for an interview for a welding position are asking or demanding a minimum of $25 per hour. Certified welders with five years of experience earn $32 to $40 per hour. Can you imagine what it would do to our shop employees when our top salary is $20 per hour for our welders? If we hire a new welder out of college with no experience at $25 or $30 per hour, we will have a total mutiny?" I asked, "Of the welders you have on staff right now, what is the average seniority?" Jonathan answered, "We have two guys that have been here for two years and four that have been here for three months."

"Once a month, one of our welders comes into my office and demands a raise, or he will leave. About 90% of the time, I give the employee a bump in salary to keep him from quitting." I asked, "Do you think that you are paying the welders under the current market for welders? These shop guys always talk with each other and know they have leverage over you. They know that if they threaten to leave the company and find a new job, you will give them a raise in salary to keep them from leaving! As long as you try to pay these guys a salary under the current market for the position, you will probably have employee turnover every month. The problem with employee turnover is that the more you have, the more you will have. When an employee leaves for more money, all the welders will seek the same position." Jonathan again had that stressful look and asked me, "So, tell me, Mr. Consultant, how do we solve this problem and still make a profit?" I responded, "I am not prepared to answer your question on my first day visiting your business. But I promise you, before I leave here, I will have that problem solved!" *(See PIR #9 on page #89.)*

I sat at the big conference room table in Suzanne's office and wrote comprehensive notes about everything I saw and learned about the company today, representing problems. At 4:00 p.m., Suzanne walked into the office to tell me she was leaving to drive home and asked if I needed a ride to my hotel. Jonathan had offered me a company jeep to use while I was in Utah rather than paying for a rental car. I thought the loaner Jeep would not happen on this trip. I packed my computer in my backpack and was in Suzanne's Bronco within three minutes. Fifteen minutes later, Suzanne dropped me off at my hotel. She asked, "Bob, are we doing breakfast again tomorrow morning?" I answered, "Same time and place tomorrow morning as today works for me!" She responded, "See you in the morning, and I hope you get a great night's sleep." I smiled, jumped out of the vehicle, and headed to my room.

When I got to my room, it was around 4:30 p.m., meaning it was too early to go to dinner. I quickly showered and pulled out my hand-written notes from today's breakfast meeting. I sat at the desk to add more notes until 6:30 p.m.. Then, I planned to go downstairs to the restaurant and have a little dinner. I did not have lunch today, so by 6:30 p.m., I was sure I would be ready to fill my stomach with healthy food. Sitting in a hotel room has never been my favorite, so I decided to go to the hotel lobby and find a quiet place to update all my notes. It was ideal when I got to the lobby with my notes and laptop. No one was hanging around the lobby, and the room was quiet, so I could concentrate to recap my day. I found an empty table in the corner by the big picture window in the lobby, with a view of Main Street. The table was perfect because the window gave me great natural light to work in.

I opened my laptop and pulled up one of the blank Daily Billing Recap – "DBR" forms where I always post my daily time on the job and a recap of all the notes from the day. Whenever I finish a consulting engagement, I have a DBR form completed for every day that I am either on-site at the client's facility or if I am working at home and have "Zoom" meetings with the client. I have always felt I should keep perfect records of my time and work for every client. Before I go to bed every night when I am on the road, I always have my DBR completed for that client for that day. I also complete a "Profit Improvement Recommendation form – "PIR" on any problems I find during the day. This consulting job has been the exception of any turnaround I have ever worked on since I started doing turnarounds. On the first day of this engagement, I could and did a write-up of nine PIRs. Never have I discovered and written five PIRs on the first day of a turnaround consulting engagement in 25 years of consulting.

PIR #8 – Meet with the owner and management team of the powder coating vendor to discuss and improve the quality of their services. (Responsible Party – Jonathan)

Observation: The powder coating company needs to deliver better quality of its services. Twenty percent of the bumpers failed the inspection of the powder coating process due to paint runs and discoloring.

Conclusion: This problem is causing a severe slowdown in the production and shipping of our bumpers. This powder coating issue is one of the problems causing the 26-week backlog of customer orders. The vendor must correct this problem immediately; Utah Off-road must find a new vendor or both.

PIR Rating: I rate this problem as seven out of ten.

Action Plan: The company must accomplish the following:

1. The employee responsible for picking up the finished product from the powder coating vendor should inspect the bumpers on-site rather than bring all the bumpers back to Utah Off-road and send back the bumpers with a quality problem. (Completed on 8/11/20XX)

2. The employees doing the inspections on the powder coating quality should start keeping accurate records of the number of bumpers that did not pass the inspection. (Completed on 8/11/20XX)

3. Jonathan should meet with the owner and senior manager on-site at the powder coating operation to discuss and resolve the problems. (Completed on 8/11/20XX)

4. Jonathan needs to accurately calculate the accumulated cost that the powder coating errors are costing Utah Off-road and agree with the owner on how he will reimburse Jonathan's company for those errors. (Completed on 8/11/20XX)

5. Jonathan needs to research and find an alternative powder coating company to use if his existing company can't fix its problems. (Completed on 8/11/20XX)

6. Jonathan should search for a new powder coating company in the area. He should meet with the owner, do a tour of the company, and determine if the new company can powder coat the quality and quantity of bumpers that Utah Off-road will need to do soon after they experience sub stantial sales growth from all the changes to the operations in the shop as stated in the PIRs. (Completed on 8/11/20XX)

7. If the new vendor proves acceptable, Jonathan should split the number of bumpers in half and use both powder coating companies in the immediate future. (Completed on 8/11/20XX)

Financial Benefit: Resolving this problem would create an annual economic benefit of $50,000.

Deadline to Complete: August 31, 20XX

PIR #9 – Research the current market salary for welders in the Salt Lake City area and adjust the hourly shop wages to reduce the constant turnover of the employees. (Responsible Party – Jonathan and Suzanne)

Observation: Jonathan has attempted to keep the salaries as low as possible by paying the employees in the shop and office 29% to 37% below the market compensation for the positions. This policy has created excessive employee turnover because the employees can easily find new positions at a higher hourly rate. Employee turnover is one of the most expensive business expenses because when an employee leaves the company, it causes:

1. A reduction in productivity in the shop, therefore causing an increase in the backlog of shipping customer orders,

2. The additional cost to recruit and hire the new replacement employees,

3. The added cost associated with training the new employees,

4. Poor employee morale from the existing employees due to the additional workload and the loss of a fellow worker,

5. Poor image and reputation of the management team to the employees due to the high volume of employee turnover,

6. Employee turnover causes more employee turnover,

7. It takes a lot of the management's time to recruit, interview, hire, onboard, and train a new employee, which would not be necessary if the company paid its welders the market salary rate.

Conclusion: Jonathan and Suzanne must research other manufacturing companies inside their industrial development to determine the average hourly rates for certified welders and shop employees. They should also google to investigate the current average certified welder wages in Salt Lake City.

PIR Rating: I rate this issue as eight out of ten.

Action Plan: Once the company determines a competitive hourly wage for certified welders from the research,

1. The owners should give all the certified welders a performance review. Jonathan should adjust the welders' pay to the minimum hourly wage for the area's certified welders. (Completed on 9/30/20XX)

2. Jonathan and Suzanne should check the average wages for a new welder who has just graduated from the area's trade schools and has five years of experience. (Completed on 9/30/20XX)

3. The owners or shop supervisor should do performance reviews every six months for the certified welders and make the appropriate salary adjustments. (Completed on 9/30/20XX)

Financial Benefit: Employee turnover is an expensive problem in this company. For this PIR, it will improve cash flow and profitability by $50,000 per year.

Deadline to Complete: September 30, 20XX

Chapter 5

YOU MUST HAVE A PLAN!

"An idiot with a plan can beat a genius without a plan."
— WARREN BUFFETT – AN AMERICAN BUSINESS MAGNATE, INVESTOR AND PHILANTHROPIST

Tuesday, August 9th – Day 2 of week 1 of the turnaround engagement

MY 8:00 A.M. SCHEDULED BREAKFAST WITH MY new clients started when they arrived at 8:30 a.m. Yes, that is right, 8:30, not 8:00 a.m. By then, I was starting on my second cup of coffee! I stood up and reached out my right hand to shake hands with Jonathan when he and Suzanne came to sit at the table. Jonathan said, "Good morning, Bob. You do not have to get up; it is only Suzanne and me. So, what did you think about your first day at our company?"

I thought, 'Boy, is that a loaded question!' I had to make a quick decision on how to answer Jonathan. My unfiltered answer would have been that the company is a total mess! Jonathan has been very defensive so far because he is insecure about managing this company profitably. Not only is he self-doubting, but I believe he does not like working at or managing this company. Jonathan does not enjoy being here because this owner knows he is not good at it. He has been unsuccessfully trying to sell the company for the past three-plus years so he could have only one job after the sale, designing new bumpers for the company's new owners. Jonathan is an engineer and loves creating the products that their company sells. Designing the bumpers and other offroad products is his sweet spot. He is not a leader and does not want to be responsible for the success or failure of Utah Off-road.

Brian, the owner of ABC Off-road Supply, shared information about Jonathan's skills, abilities, wants, and needs with me. We talked on the phone right before starting the turnaround engagement. Brian and Jonathan have known each other for many years, and Brian has tried to mentor Jonathan. After I turned around Brian's company a year ago to be extraordinarily profitable, Brian's ego about his ability to manage a company successfully is up in the clouds now, which is a good thing! Unfortunately, Jonathan is too stubborn to let someone like Brian help mentor him. I am afraid that includes me, too. I am guessing time will tell if I am right about that opinion.

I decided to go with the conservative route with my response. I said, "I enjoyed the entire day yesterday. I noted several opportunities in your company that we could tweak and improve your business's cash flow and profitability. It is my first impression on seeing the operations that you are managing the company with extremely conservative business decisions. I understand your conservative route to protect the business, the cash flow, and most importantly, your family!" I did not tell him my management style is the opposite; I am extremely aggressive when managing a business. The stressed look on Jonathan's face relaxed when he heard my answer. I aim to get Jonathan to relax and be open to me so I can help improve his business.

Based on my first day's notes from the tour and our conversations, there are a lot of opportunities to make some quick, inexpensive, and easy changes to the business. We will see an immediate reduction in the backlog report's 26 weeks of customer orders. I plan to do everything possible to get all the work-in-process inventory clogging up the shop's aisles finished and shipped as soon as possible to the respective customers. If we increased the speed of the fabrication processes, it would reduce the number of weeks we would have to tell our customers that it would take them to receive their offroad product orders. Without any doubt, when this company reduces the time from the customers' order date to the shipment date to a more reasonable time, it would materially increase their annual sales. I continued, "Your company is losing sales as soon as the customer learns that they will have to wait six months to receive the product they ordered. It would also reduce each bumper's labor cost, increasing the gross profit of every product shipped. Both results (increased sales and increase in the gross profit of each bumper) would have a definite positive impact on the company's profitability and cash flow."

I shared with the two owners, "Last night in my room, after Suzanne dropped me off at the hotel, I showered and went downstairs for dinner. I had a couple of cups of coffee with dinner. I wanted to be wide awake and able to work for three- or four additional hours. I planned to develop my turnaround plan based upon my first day's information at your company's facility."

In my past 25 years of doing turnarounds, I do not remember any clients with so many obvious problems and issues needing immediate attention. Being able to develop a lengthy list of absolute problems after my first eight hours at my client's facility was not close to normal. These were all obvious material problems with its operations in the showroom and shop. These problems are so evident that I need to understand why the owners have yet to fix the issues themselves. The answer was obvious: they have yet to gain business education or experience managing a $3,200,000 company. Managing a multi-million-dollar company is easier when the owner has a business education, experience, and training. I have yet to dig into the office operations, but I am sure that when I do, it will turn out to be a mess, too. The question is, why wouldn't it be?

I continued, "After dinner, I returned to my room, got my computer out, and started writing. I did not turn the television on because I had so much on my mind and in my notes about the tour of the facilities and our conversations. When I started working, I wanted zero distractions. I first wrote an outline of all the issues I wanted to put in the turnaround plan. *(See the outline on page #97 and #98.)* When I completed the outline, I planned to start writing rough drafts of the PIRs. I describe the problems by documenting my observations, conclusions, and action plans to resolve each major problem. I want to share some of them with the two of you one day this week while I am still in Utah. After I finish writing the rough draft of one of the PIRs, I save it. I review it later to recheck and verify my thoughts about each problem. By doing this, I am double-checking my work before I share it with both of you. I do this and then start making changes to the company. I then prioritize each problem on my outline by which we should attack and fix each problem (first, second, etc.)."

"Per my notes, the first item on the plan was to find a computer programmer who could program the four dust collectors and get them operating immediately. Oops, I meant the two robotic welders and the two robotic grinders in the shop."

After doing a little research about the problem, I could not believe solving this problem was as tough as Jonathan was making it. With the commitment from the equipment company that sold Jonathan the robots several months ago that they would reimburse the company for hiring a third-party programmer, the cost to resolve this problem is a non-issue. I will solve this problem by using someone else's wallet.

I continued sharing my thoughts with Jonathan and Suzanne, "My first option to solve this problem would be to visit Weber State University ("WSU"). I researched last night and discovered that WSU has a program in Manufacturing Engineering Technology (Bachelor of Science degree) with a welding emphasis. The WSU campus is only seven miles from Utah Off-road. That is an ideal location to find some welders who are studying and will graduate soon to be certified welders. "Per my research, all the program's students must take computer programming classes for robotic welders and grinders. Those students are ideal for the positions we need to fill in the shop."

Utah Off-road, Inc.
Turnaround Outline
As of 8/8/20XX

Improve shop operations.

1. The 26-week order backlog is hurting the company's sales.

2. The robotic welders and grinders in the shop need programming to start operating. We need a computer programmer to program these four pieces of equipment.

3. Based on the current customer order volume, the under-staffed shop is hurting the company.

4. Currently, there is no shop supervision which is hurting production.

5. The pay scale for the welders is materially below the market value of certified welders, causing a turnover that is hurting the production of the business.

6. The owners must add a second production shift to reduce the backlog of open customer orders.

7. The powder coating vendor has a 20% error factor. This problem needs resolving, or the client should find a new vendor for the future.

8. The shop does not have safety policies or a procedure manual.

9. The owner's 17-year-old son should not be working in the shop.

10. There must be installation instructions written for all of the offroad products sold.

Improve shop and office environment.

1. Clean the showroom, shop, offices, vehicles, and bathrooms.

2. Finish designing and installing the offroad products for the vehicles in the showroom.

Improve business operations and office environment.

1. Don't purchase vehicles to install the newly designed offroad bumpers in the future. Instead, sell the offroad bumpers to the car dealerships and profit from the transaction.

2. The two owners must familiarize themselves with GAAP or federal income tax regulations regarding fixed assets and depreciation.

3. The tax preparer should audit the prior year's tax returns.

I continued, "Jonathan, I have another couple of ideas about how nice it is having a university like WSU close that can help your company. We may be able to hire one of the instructors from WSU who will teach the students computer programming classes for the welding and grinding robots. Because college instructors, especially the ones who are adjunct professors, receive nominal salaries for teaching classes, one may be available. It will be easier to find a programmer at the university to do the programming for our robots." *(See PIR #10 on page #115.)*

"As you are aware, I was the CFO of the college that my wife was the president of for many years. Because I have my master's degree in taxation, the vice president of education asked me if I would teach two tax classes. The college had an instructor leave suddenly, and they needed someone to replace the professor for these two tax courses. I agreed to help and teach the classes. I am surprised how little instructors earn when they are only adjunct professors.

There are only two categories of college professors: adjunct and full-time. The full-time instructors' salaries are okay, depending on the number of years that they have been teaching. The compensation is so low for adjunct instructors that they must have a second full-time job to pay their bills and feed their families. They either teach for a little extra money or love the college atmosphere and teaching students."

"Jonathan, when we meet with the head administrator at WSU responsible for the Manufacturing Engineering Technology program, we can discuss another idea I have. We should tell him that Utah Off-road would like to start an internship for their students in their welding program. An intern program would be a wonderful win–win opportunity for your company and the university. You can have WSU students here working in your shop, producing offroad bumpers with no labor cost. They, the university, can have their students in a real-life, practical corporate welding shop for college credit. All the students enrolled in our intern program would be great candidates for your company. We could hire them as full-time employees (welders) after completing the intern program requirements and graduating from *WSU*. Your company can cherry-pick the best students from the intern program." Jonathan spoke up again enthusiastically, "Bob, I love that idea, too. Our company is in a win-win situation with the welding intern program idea."

Suzanne asked, "Bob, do you know how to run a college intern program? We have no experience in anything like that. I would never get involved with an intern program at the university unless it was well-planned and a positive experience for all the college students in the internship." I quickly responded to Suzanne's comment, "Suzanne and Jonathan, trust me, I would never suggest anything that there is any chance the two of you would crash and burn with the program. First, my wife is president of a five-campus college in Florida. The college has dozens of students in internship programs. Also, with all the other companies in the industrial park, I would not be surprised if WSU has students enrolled in welding internship programs with one or more of these other companies." Suzanne responded, "Bob, you are right. Can we check into this before starting an intern program for this company?" I finished the conversation by telling Suzanne, "Of course!" *(See PIR #11 on page #117.)*

"Please let me explain my view of your company and the current condition that it is in. Let's start with the shop staff. The company's shop needs more staff and productivity based on the number of sales or customer orders you receive. That is clear to me based on your 26-week order backlog. Several issues are causing that order backlog."

1. First, there needs to be more supervision in the shop to oversee the staff production.

2. Right now, the people who work in your shop need to have written company rules or procedures to follow. There are no operating manuals or written procedures at any fabrication station.

3. The employee turnover in the shop could be better. Half the six or seven people working on manufacturing bumpers have been here less than six months. In the other half, no one has three years of seniority yet. When any of these employees in the shop leave, the costs that this company invested in the training and experience they have received in your shop leave with them.

4. When I walk into your shop, it is easy to tell that there are no signs that note any safety policies or procedures in the workplace. These welders are carrying around these heavy bumpers without any back belts. If one of your welders hurts his back carrying one of these heavy bumpers, he will be out of work for a long time collecting on a workers' compensation insurance claim. You lose a valuable worker that you must replace. Also, your workers' compensation insurance premiums will increase due to worker claims.

5. Next, there needs to be operating statistics or data to see how well or poorly each employee produces in the shop. Peter Drucker was an American writer, professor,

management consultant, and author who wrote 39 business books. He contributed to the theory and practice of modern business and management. Peter is known for a famous quote that fits very well here at your company. "If you can't measure it, you can't improve it."[1] This quote means: "*One can only know whether or not you are successful if success is defined and you track it regularly.*" With a clearly understood measurement system for success, you can measure progress and change your process to produce the desired result. Without clear objectives, you're caught in endless guessing."

I continued, "When I was in the shop yesterday, I did not see anyone tracking the output of their work. Let me share with you my thoughts about the measurement of output.

If you see a Utah Jazz basketball game, what do they put up on the scoreboard in bright lights? They put up statistics about the score of each team, the time clock, the number of points per player, the number of personal fouls for each player, etc. When you look on the ESPN.com website and see the basketball game results, they list stats for many categories for every player and team. The statistics include minutes played, field goals attempted and made, three-point shots attempted and made, free throw shots attempted and made, offensive rebounds, defensive rebounds, total rebounds, assists, steals, blocks, turnovers, personal fouls, plus / minus total, and the total points. The teams and media would only spend the time and effort collecting and displaying all those statistics if it were important. Statistics help motivate the players to become better basketball players. The statistics support the players getting larger salaries when their numbers are better. When

---

1 Peter Drucker – Drucker Institute

the team's statistics are better, the team wins more. When the team wins more, the team's owners make more money, money from the company's profits."

"The reason this company should keep statistics on the productivity of each employee and the total shop is that the more productive the shop is, the more profits the business will produce. The more profits the company makes, the more money the owners make. When a company keeps statistics for employees, they are more motivated to work harder and be more productive."

The statistics create a sense of competition for the group in the shop, making every employee more productive. The more effective the shop is, the quicker we can ship bumpers to customers. The quicker the shop sends the bumpers to the customers; the customer order backlog will start going down from the current level of 26 weeks to somewhere around two to three weeks. We must post the productivity statistics daily or weekly on a bulletin board in the shop. Every employee who works here can see how he is doing productivity-wise compared to the rest of the group. I have used this strategy with other clients, especially the sales force.

We would have a sales meeting every Friday afternoon, and on the whiteboard in the sales conference room, we would have posted on the board the weekly, monthly, and quarterly sales results by a salesperson. We listed the sales results on the board, from the top salesperson's results to the person with the weakest sales results. This process always motivated each person on the sales team. The person on top would continue to work hard to produce strong results and stay on top of the ranking list. The salespeople at the top of the report make more sales commissions. The people at the bottom of the list with the least sales would be embarrassed and automatically work harder to get off the bottom. This process was a win–win procedure for everyone. When the sales team does better, the sales staff makes more money, as does the company."

"To enhance the shop's staff motivation, we should develop a productivity commission plan for the group. If the people in the shop make more money when they are more productive, I promise they will produce and ship more bumpers than they are today."

"Motivating the sales force to get more sales using the minimal time and effort from the management team (posting the sales results on the whiteboard) helped grow the sales, and the company made more profits. The salespeople would work harder, grow their sales, and earn more commissions."

I continued, "After we have met with the WSU people, if we are not successful there, we need to get online with the different employment websites such as Indeed or ZipRecruiter. We must find a programmer anywhere near your facilities, preferably in Utah. We will pay their fee and travel expenses to get to Utah on the next flight to resolve this programming problem as soon as possible. The employment internet websites would be a backup insurance plan for us to find a programmer with the knowledge to program our robots! But my gut tells me that the WSU people will allow us to find the perfect candidate to resolve our computer programming problems with the four robots. Whatever the cost is for the programmer's time to complete the project, I would happily pay it, even at a premium hourly rate. The cost is not important because of the reimbursement by the equipment manufacturer. The critical issue is to get those four robots in the shop operating efficiently and do it soon. That is the first item listed on my plan, and obviously, the most important because of the material cost saving and increased production issues."

"The second item on my list is to train an employee to program these robots in the future. Having an instructor from WSU is ideal because the cost of that individual would be minimal compared to the financial benefits. After the robots work properly, this company needs to have someone on staff to keep them working. If we are lucky enough to find an instructor from WSU, that person can be responsible for training one or two of our existing employees to be the backup programmer."

"A computer programmer for maintaining the welding and grinding robots is valuable to have employed at Utah Off-road because the robots will significantly reduce the labor cost of each bumper. The robots that will weld/grind the bumpers four times faster than any human welder are extremely valuable to this business. If these four machines are running efficiently, the programmer would be worth his weight in gold."

"My vision is for the robots to operate two or three eight-hour daily shifts. The robots continue operating around the clock until the existing work-in-process inventory is gone. According to my calculations, if the company had the programming done and four certified welders to supervise these four robotic machines, a material portion of the company's production problems would disappear. Labor-wise, it would take two employees per shift, one for the two welders and one for the two grinders – for two shifts per day, five days a week. These four machines could accomplish more production in two shifts, five-day workweeks than the existing staff in six weeks. When these robots are operating properly, the total labor cost per bumper would be approximately one-third compared to today's cost per bumper under the existing procedures."

"The Utah Off-road website has a dropdown message indicating that the backlog of bumper customer orders is 26 weeks. If I was going to personally order a product on the internet from this company and the message on the website stated that I would have to pay for the product today, then I would expect that the product would ship within two to three weeks. But, if the message were that I would not receive the product for six months, I would start searching for another company to buy the product. Many companies design and manufacture offroad products like your bumpers in the aftermarket industry. The fact is, I don't know how many sales your company is losing because of the 26-week backlog of customer orders. It is difficult to determine what that sales increase would be. We must get the backorders down to two or three weeks, change the order lead time notice on the website, and watch future customer orders double or triple from the current sales order level. This company has a poor reputation with its customers because of the long backlog problem."

"Once we make the improvements to reduce the long lead times to ship the customer orders, we will need to do some marketing to make the public aware that this company is now shipping their orders in two to three weeks. We will put a banner notification on the first page of the website so that is the first thing our customers see – 'Utah Off-road is now shipping their customer orders within two to three weeks of the customer order date.' We should also buy ads on social media to make the public aware that Utah Off-road is now shipping all orders within 30 days of the order date. Since the company has maintained a database of customers who have purchased products from this company, we should develop a marketing email and send it to all those customers."

"We will need a contingency plan in case we get many orders once we announce our shorter order-to-ship time. We want the company to always tell the customers the truth and live up to our promises." With Jonathan and Suzanne sitting at the breakfast table staring at me, I continued, "When I develop a turnaround business plan for a client, I first list my goals before I list the actual tasks to accomplish. So far, the most important goal is to reduce the backlog from 26 weeks to two or three weeks. That, I am sure, is what the two of you want and are paying me for."

"When the sales volume increases because of the reduced order backlog time, the company should recruit and hire additional certified welders who have experience with using robotic welders and grinders. It is a proven fact that robots are much faster than human welders and less than two-thirds the labor cost. The company aims to keep the backlog of orders between two and three weeks. Suppose the sales volume materially increases once the company is shipping bumpers two or three weeks after receiving the orders, Jonathan. In that case, consider adding a third shift in the shop to run the robots 24 hours a day, five or even seven days per week."

I added, "Once we fix the problems with the robots, I have other thoughts on improving the production in the shop."

1. Hire a strong supervisor to manage all the employees working in the shop. The supervisor should be a certified welder and have experience managing a shop that uses welding and grinding robots.

2. When the company hires a second shift to process the orders, we must have a supervisor in the shop. Jonathan,

you should be able to share the responsibility with the new supervisor if you oversee the shop in the mornings from 7:00 a.m. to 3:00 p.m., and the new supervisor's position will work from 3:00 p.m. to 11:00 p.m. That will provide a manager on-site in the shop at least 16 hours per day." *(See PIR #12 on page #119.)*

3. "When we produce more bumpers quicker, we will need more laborers in the shop to move the bumpers through each fabrication process. The welders that we pay between $20 to $30 per hour are too expensive to have them do the work of a $12 to $15 per hour basic laborer. We should have the welders welding 100% of the time in the shop and not moving the bumpers around the shop. If we have one or two laborers moving the bumpers between fabrication stations, the production of the welders would materially increase. The more production we get from our welders, the quicker we manufacture the bumpers, reducing our customer order backlog." *(See PIR #13 on page #120.)*

4. Create a chart of the organization listing all the new hires and staff positions. *(See the Chart of Organizations – "Existing" and "Proposed" on pages #110 and #111.)*

Because of the apparent employee turnover problem, Jonathan and Suzanne need to upgrade their policies and procedures regarding employee relations and compensation. I have not been at the company long enough to grade their performance in these areas. Employee relations and compensation are critical areas they could improve because of the substantial number of employees leaving the company.

Onboarding is one of the most critical areas in the employee relations area. "Onboarding" a new employee is not simple to accomplish, but it is essential. The onboarding process should start as early as possible, even before the employee starts the job. Ideally, onboarding should begin immediately after the candidate receives an offer letter and continue for at least a month after the new hire starts the job. Once the candidate has accepted the position, signed the offer letter, and passed the background check and drug tests, the company should prepare for the start date for the new employee. Suzanne will immediately assign the future employee a company email address, phone number, and professional cards. The candidate's workspace must be ready to make the employee feel at home on the first day.

Utah Off-road, Inc.
Existing Chart of Organization
As of August 8, 20XX

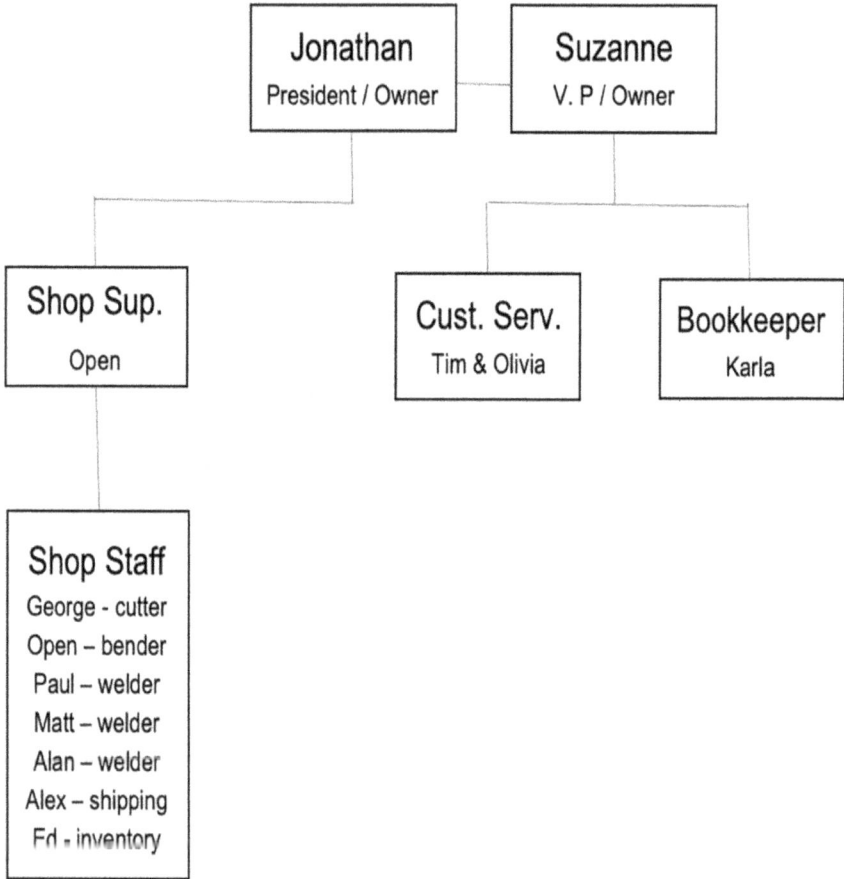

Jonathan	Suzanne
President / Owner	V. P / Owner

Shop Sup.

Open

Cust. Serv.

Tim & Olivia

Bookkeeper

Karla

Shop Staff

George - cutter
Open – bender
Paul – welder
Matt – welder
Alan – welder
Alex – shipping
Fd - inventory

Utah Off-road, Inc.
Proposed Chart of Organization
As of August 8, 20XX

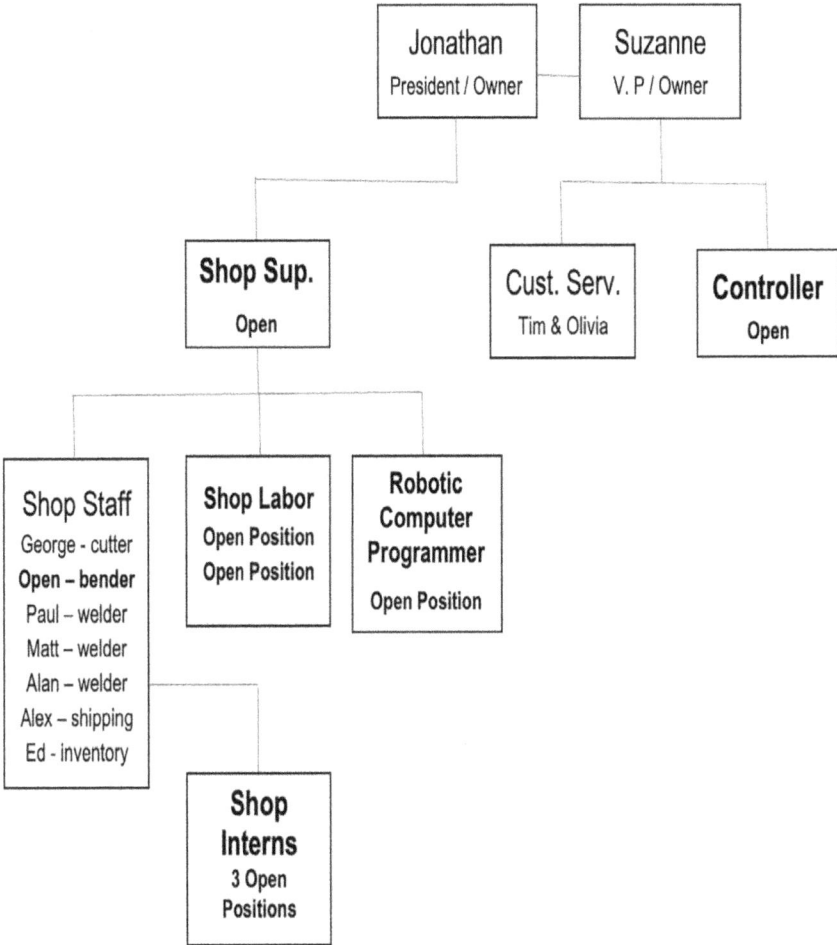

```
┌─────────────────┐   ┌─────────────────┐
│    Jonathan     │   │    Suzanne      │
│ President/Owner │   │  V. P / Owner   │
└─────────────────┘   └─────────────────┘
```

Shop Sup.
Open

Cust. Serv.
Tim & Olivia

Controller
Open

Shop Staff
George - cutter
Open – bender
Paul – welder
Matt – welder
Alan – welder
Alex – shipping
Ed - inventory

Shop Labor
Open Position
Open Position

Robotic Computer Programmer
Open Position

Shop Interns
3 Open Positions

An excellent onboarding policy is to send the new hire a photograph of each member of the existing management team and the candidate's future direct reports with bios for each employee. This procedure makes their first day on the job much more comfortable. When introducing the new employee to the managers and employees, the new hire will have a much easier time remembering faces and names. Also, during the introduction, always highlight the new hire's strengths and business experience. Everything shared during the conversation should be positive to help the new hire feel comfortable.

It is also a promising idea to assign a mentor to the new hire. The mentor should be another manager or a long-term employee from the same department as the new employee. The mentoring employee should check in with the new employee regularly to help increase the new hire's comfort level with the company's corporate culture.

The company's employees need to welcome the new hire. When hiring a new manager, each senior management team member should allocate a few hours to sit and talk with the new person in the first few days.

The president/owner of the company, especially if the new person is an accounting manager or controller, should schedule lunches in the first month with the latest management team member. The president should ask other managers to join the lunches, breaking the ice for the new employee. Every company, small or large, should have a strong onboarding process to hire new employees successfully.

"We should implement an incentive bonus plan for the shop employees to reward the staff for increased production. There are several positive factors with a well-thought-out incentive plan that includes both an improvement in the quality and the quantity of the output. Many positive things can happen to your company's sales and profits when your production increases without increasing your shop staff. The goal is to produce the bumpers quickly with top quality work."

"The incentive plan is based upon the production of the whole shop rather than each fabrication station by station. When a company has a reward system based on the shop's output, it creates a "teamwork" atmosphere. If there is a weak staff worker in the shop, the other employees will find a solution to the problem rather than let that one or two employees negatively impact their monthly bonus. The process is self-policing by every employee in the shop."

"Currently, there is no reporting of statistical operations information about the production in the shop. Effective immediately, we will gather production statistics, maintain them, and report them weekly, monthly, and quarterly. The owners, management team, and shop supervisors must use the data to motivate and reward the shop employees. The management team will review the prior week's data every Friday late afternoon. At that time, they will develop new goals for the next couple of weeks. We will post the weekly data on the conference room whiteboard so everyone can easily see whether the production is improving."

"After we gather one month's statistics, we will create the incentive program goals and share them with the shop staff. The management team should develop different tiers of incentive rewards for the staff. In other words, the more the shop staff produces, the bigger the monthly incentive. There should be no limits to the amount of the reward payments."
(See PIR #14 on page #122.)

I added, "And Jonathan, per our earlier discussion, we will include the newly written installation instructions with each customer shipment in the future. I am sure nothing would be more frustrating to your customers if they finally receive their offroad bumper order from Utah Off-road and do not have any installation instructions with the shipment." Jonathan answered, "I have that on my new to-do list! You don't understand how long it takes to do just one set of bumper installation instructions!" I said: "But Jonathan, how many customers have called and complained to your customer service department since you have not been sending installation instructions with your shipments of your bumpers?" Suzanne spoke up, "90% Bob. We have some very frustrated customers out there!" *(See PIR #15 on page #123.)*

We finished our breakfast meeting, discussing all the work we needed to accomplish, and then drove to the Utah Off-road facility. After our morning conversation, I knew I had a lot of writing to do. Documenting, organizing, and prioritizing all the work to complete is my priority. Because of Jonathan's and Suzanne's lack of business knowledge and experience, each task would be twice as tough to finish as it would be if they were "seasoned" business owners.

Once we got to the facility, I went to Suzanne's office to work on all my notes and turnaround outline.

When I entered Suzanne's office, there was a copy of each of my three books on the conforonoc room table. I put down my backpack and picked up the books. They all looked used like someone had read them several times. Suzanne walked into the office behind me and said, "Bob, George asked me yesterday if it was okay if he brought his copy of your books in to get you to sign each of them. I told him that it was okay." I answered, "When I met George yesterday during the shop tour at the cutting machine, he asked me if he brought in his copies of my books, would I sign them for him, and I said that I would love to sign each of them for him!" I sat at the table, signed them all "George, Go with Confidence," then signed my name with the date below. I then took them out to the shop to return them to George! When I handed them to him, he was extremely grateful! Hmm, what a nice guy!

I spent the rest of the day sitting at the conference room table, documenting all the changes I wanted to make to this company to take it From Losses to Profits!

Profit Improvement Recommendations

PIR #10 – Recruit one of the adjunct instructors from WSU with programming knowledge to come to the company and do the required computer programming to get all the robotic machines working properly. (Responsible Party – Jonathan)

Observation: The company's welding and grinding robots have never worked since Jonathan purchased the equipment about six months ago. When Jonathan bought the machines, the vendor sent an employee to program the robots' computers and failed. The vendor offered Jonathan to hire a third-party programmer. The equipment vendor committed to reimburse Utah Off-road for the cost of the programmer to do the necessary programming to get the machines operating. Jonathan needs to put more time and effort into finding a programmer to get the four machines running. Once these machines are functioning properly, there will be a huge increase in the shop's productivity, positively impacting cash flow and the company's profits.

Conclusion: The company, and when I say, "the company," I really mean Jonathan, should immediately put the effort into successfully finding and hiring a qualified computer programmer to do the required programming to each robotic machine to get them all operating efficiently.

PIR Rating: I rate this PIR a ten out of ten.

Action Plan:

1. To find a qualified programmer, Jonathan should check with Weber State University, which offers a Manufacturing Engineering Technology program with a welding emphasis. All students in this program take computer programming classes to earn their degrees and graduate. (Completed on 8/19/20XX)

2. Suppose Jonathan can negotiate consulting or part-time employment with one of the instructors at WSU to program the robots in his shop. In that case, he should have the instructors come to do the programming as soon as possible to get all four pieces of equipment operating immediately. (Completed on 8/19/20XX)

3. Once the instructor completes the required programming to get the equipment operating properly, Suzanne will submit the cost paid to the consultant for reimbursement by the equipment vendor. (Completed on 8/19/20XX)

Financial Benefit: Once the company can find a computer programmer to get these four pieces of equipment to operate, the economic benefit will be huge for the company's cash flow and profitability. For this PIR, it will improve cash flow and profitability by a minimum of $100,000 annually.

Deadline to Complete: August 31, 20XX

PIR #11 – Meet with the head of the manufacturing engineering technology program at WSU and offer the university a welding intern program at Utah Off-road. (Responsible Party – Jonathan and Suzanne)

Observation: Utah Off-road has a shortage of shop staff caused by underpaying the welders compared to the market salary wages for certified welders, no shop supervision, and poor working conditions for the existing team.

The WSU is only seven miles from the company and has a Manufacturing Engineering Technology program that could be beneficial to find and hire certified welding candidates.

Conclusion: Utah Off-road should work with the head administrator at WSU to offer the university an internship program for welding. The internship for the students at WSU could benefit the university and Utah Off-road.

PIR Rating: I rate this PIR seven out of ten.

Action Plan:

1. In cooperation with WSU, Jonathan, and Suzanne should design a formal intern program for students to work at their shop for at least one semester to learn all the technical steps to create an offroad bumper. Then, the students

should learn how to build the product in their facility. The students would gain experience working at all the stations, including bending, cutting, welding, grinding, welding 2, powder coating, and shipping. (Completed on 12/31/20XX)

2. Jonathan should schedule a meeting with the head of the Manufacturing Engineering Technology program to offer the students in the program the chance to participate in the internship. During this meeting, Jonathan should ask and understand what the university needs from the company once the students have completed the training. (Completed on 12/31/20XX)

3. Jonathan should review all the safety policies and pro-cedures in the shop and upgrade them where necessary before the intern program starts. (Completed on 8/31/20XX)

4. Once Weber State, Jonathan, and Suzanne approve the program, they should all have a group meeting with the whole shop staff to explain the intern program and describe the employees' role once it starts. (Completed on 12/31/20XX)

Financial Benefit: There are great benefits once the company establishes a relationship with WSU and has students working for an intern program at Utah Off-road. One of the benefits would be lowering the average labor cost of each bumper shipped. They would also have a valuable resource for recruiting and hiring staff for the shop. For this PIR, it will improve cash flow and profitability by $50,000 per year.

Deadline to Complete: December 31, 20XX

PIR #12 – Hire a strong supervisor to manage all the employees working in the shop directly. (Responsible Party – Jonathan and Suzanne)

Observation: Currently, the shop needs a supervisor overseeing the operations of the shop. Jonathan spends little time in the shop during the workday because he dislikes supervising people. With no supervision in the shop, the staff works at a much lower production rate.

Conclusion: The company should hire a shop supervisor as soon as possible to oversee all daily operations, including the computer programming of the robotic welders and grinders, the hiring and firing of shop staff, the safety conditions in the facility, and keeping the daily production up at each fabrication station.

PIR Rating: I rate this PIR a nine out of ten.

Action Plan:

1. Jonathan should research the current market salary for a shop supervisor for a manufacturer in the Salt Lake City geographic area who would be responsible for managing more than ten employees. (Completed on 10/31/20XX)

2. Jonathan should develop a job description including the salary range for the position. *(See pages #125 to #127 for an example of a shop supervisor job description.) (See page #128 for an example of a job offer letter for a shop supervisor.)* The candidate should have computer programming experience for robotic welders and grinders. (Completed on 10/31/20XX)

3. Jonathan and Suzanne should recruit and hire a shop supervisor to work either the first shift (7:00 a.m. to 3:00 p.m.) or the second (3:00 p.m. to 11:00 p.m.) until the customer backlog is down to two to three weeks. Once selecting the candidate, Suzanne should provide him with an offer letter with all the terms and conditions of his employment. (Completed on 10/31/20XX)

4. After finding and hiring a strong candidate, Jonathan should spend at least four hours per day for the first two weeks with the supervisor to provide him with an "onboarding" program to introduce him to the shop and all the employees who report to him. (Completed on 10/31/20XX)

Financial Benefit: For this PIR, it will improve cash flow and profitability by $50,000 per year.

Deadline to Complete: September 30, 20XX

PIR #13 – Hire two laborers in the shop to move products around to each fabrication station so the welders can focus 100% of their time on welding. (Responsible Party – Jonathan and Suzanne)

Observation: Currently, the welders working in the shop are responsible for staging the bumpers in their welding area and then moving them to the next station once they complete their welding of each bumper.

Conclusion: The welders moving bumpers are wasting their time. They earn between $20 and $30 per hour. The company should hire two laborers at $10 to $12 per hour. Their job is to do manual jobs in the shop, like staging the bumpers for the welding. They should move the bumpers from station to station.

PIR Rating: I rate this PIR a five out of ten.

Action Plan:

1. Jonathan should write a job description for the new shop labor position and research the current local market for the salary range for the position. (Completed on 9/30/20XX)

2. Suzanne should place an ad in the local newspapers' want ad section and online with the online job recruiting websites and any job posting boards at Weber State University. (Completed on 9/30/20XX)

3. Jonathan should start interviewing to hire two laborers for the shop. Once the owners hire two candidates, the company should develop an "onboarding procedure." (Completed on 9/30/20XX)

4. One of the senior employees in the shop will oversee the activities of these two new employees until the new shop supervisor is on staff and manages all the employees. (Completed on 9/30/20XX)

Financial Benefit: For this PIR, it will improve cash flow and profitability by $50,000 per year. This PIR will also help improve the status of the order backlog from 26 weeks to help get it down to our goal of two to three weeks.

Deadline to Complete: September 30, 20XX

PIR #14 – Create a production incentive plan to incentivize and motivate the shop staff to increase the shop output and maintain the quality of the craft. (Responsible Party – Jonathan and Suzanne)

Observation: Currently, the employees in the shop need to be accountable for the daily/weekly/monthly production output level. The staff can work as slowly as they want or work hard to increase the production of the bumpers, and their compensation does not change.

Conclusion: Based on the status of the order backlog report, the production of the shop staff must increase, or the company will continue to lose customer orders. Under current shop production, it takes the company six months to deliver an order to the customers. An incentive plan for increased production and the quality of the products is one of the several changes possible to reduce the time for the company to ship the customer orders to their customers.

PIR Rating: I rate this PIR seven out of ten.

Action Plan:

1. The management team should track the production data of each fabrication station to calculate the current output baseline weekly. (Completed on 9/30/20XX)

2. After collecting the production data, create new achiev-able production goals for each station with incentive

compensation at the various production levels. Management shares the information with the shop team. Hence, they are aware of the salary increase based upon the increase in production while maintaining an elevated level of quality in their work. (Completed on 9/30/20XX)

3. Gather and analyze the data regularly to understand and maintain the quality of the incentive plan. (Completed on 9/30/20XX)

Financial Benefit: This PIR will improve production by as much as 20%, enhancing annual cash flow and profitability by $100,000 annually.

Deadline to Complete: September 30, 20XX

PIR #15 – Create installation instructions for every product sold to customers. (Responsible Party – Jonathan)

Observation: Someone hacked into the client's computers, and they lost most of their products' installation instructions.

Conclusion: Jonathan or a subcontractor, should write new installation instructions for every product that needs the instructions.

PIR Rating: I rate this PIR a nine out of ten. The high rating is because every product shipped without installation instructions causes an unhappy customer. Customer service people receive calls from these customers threatening to immediately return the product if they do not receive their instructions directly.

Action Plan:

1. Create a list of every product the company sells, indicating whether that product has installation instructions. (Completed on 8/14/20XX)

2. Match the products that do not have installation instructions into categories of products that have similar installation requirements. Then Jonathan should use the installation instructions comparable to the product needing the new instructions, making writing further instructions much easier. (Completed on 08/14/20XX)

3. Prioritize the installation instructions by doing the instructions for shipped products first. (Completed on 8/8/20XX)

4. The company should hire a third party with experience in offroad products and writing installation instructions. (Completed on 8/1/20XX)

Financial Benefit: This PIR will calm many unhappy customers after receiving installation instructions. It should improve annual cash flow and profitability by $50,000 per year.

Deadline to Complete: September 15, 20XX

SHOP SUPERVISOR

JOB DESCRIPTION

JOB TITLE: Shop Supervisor
SUPERVISOR: Jonathan

Utah Off-road manufactures high-quality offroad equipment, including winch bumpers, rock sliders, and rack systems. The company also distributes a host of offroad accessories and equipment.

MAJOR DUTIES AND RESPONSIBILITIES:

Direct staff members in the shop operations, including all production.

DETAILED DUTIES AND RESPONSIBILITIES:

1. Manage staff and maintain the highest customer satisfaction and employee engagement levels.

2. Knowledge and skills in computer programming on robotic machines.

3. Set individual goals for all staff positions with financial responsibilities.

4. Monitor staff performance to ensure the accomplishment of production goals.

5. Show employees how their contributions matter to the company's success.

6. Communicate, show recognition, and build rapport with employees.

7. Monitor employee engagement levels and know how to promote a healthy work environment.

8. Train and advise staff members on regularly improving their skills and production.

9. Establish customer satisfaction metrics, evaluate performance, and coach staff to success.

10. Keep staff overtime hours at an absolute minimum.

11. Build a plan for escalating customer complaints, resulting in quick, favorable resolutions.

12. Create an annual budget, control expenses, and meet or exceed the plan.

13. Ensure sufficient staff levels to meet ongoing customer demand and seasonal spikes.

14. Recruit, interview, hire, and on-board new employees when needed to maintain production standards.

15. Promote enthusiasm and company loyalty during daily "10-minute stand-up meetings" and individual staff conferences.

16. Conduct operations and P&L meetings with key managers to increase productivity.

17. Formalize a coaching and training program that is consistent, effective, and measurable.

18. Shape company culture by living out agreed-upon values, specifically ethics and integrity.

QUALIFICATIONS FOR THE JOB

1. **Education:** College undergraduate degree

2. **Experience:** Five – ten years' experience managing shop operations in a manufacturing environment.

OTHER:

1. Develop a proven record of accomplishment in operations.

2. Ability to inspire and lead others to attain company goals.

3. Highly organized with exceptional follow-through abilities.

4. Strong verbal and written communication.

5. Quick, sound decision-making abilities.

6. Good presentation and public speaking skills are a plus.

7. Ability to build trust and demonstrate empathy.

8. Gather, maintain, and report weekly, monthly, and quarterly production statistics for the shop operations.

August 18, 20XX

Jonathan Owner
10 Main Street
Layton, Utah 84041

Mr. Donald Smith
80 Main Street
Layton, Utah 84041

Dear Mr. Smith:

We are pleased to offer you employment at Utah Offroad, Inc. Your skills and background will be valuable assets to our manufacturing team.

Per our discussion, the position is shop supervisor in our manufacturing facility. Your position as the shop supervisor will be reporting directly to me. Your starting date will be Monday, September 1, 20XX. Please confirm that this date is an accurate understanding for both of us.

The starting salary is $78,000 per year ($1,500 per week). Our paydays are weekly, usually on Fridays. Our normal procedure is to put new employees in a ninety (90) day probationary period as noted in our employee handbook. The enclosed employee handbook outlines this information and the company policies, procedures, and medical benefits our company offers.

If you accept this offer, please sign the second copy of this letter in the space provided and return it to us. We enclosed a stamped, self-addressed envelope for your convenience.

We are pleased to offer you the position and are sure you will make a superb addition to our company. If you have any questions, please call me at any time.

Sincerely,

Jonathan Owner
Owner/President

Agreed to: _____   Date: ___/___/___
                Donald Smith

Chapter 6

PIRs, NOT PRIs!!!

"Your most unhappy customers are your greatest source of learning."
– BILL GATES – AN AMERICAN BUSINESS MAGNATE, INVESTOR, PHILANTHROPIST, AND CO-FOUNDER OF SOFTWARE GIANT MICROSOFT.

Wednesday, August 10th – Day 3 of week 1 of the turnaround engagement

IT WAS A LATE-NIGHT LAST NIGHT BECAUSE I worked past midnight in my hotel room to document all my findings during the past two days. Later today, I wanted to hand Jonathan and Suzanne the formal write-ups of my PIRs I discovered on Monday and Tuesday. I planned to fly home to Fort Lauderdale early Thursday morning, so I had a lot of work to accomplish today while I was still in Utah. My most important task before I fly home is to share all the PIRs with the owners. I aim to work with them to develop a plan to start working on all the action items listed in the PIRs. I assigned a priority rating to each of the 15 PIRs I wrote. I based the rating on how the improvement would affect the company's cash flow and profitability. My plan for Wednesday was to meet the owners for a quick breakfast to give them an overview of my work completed and the PIRs. Then, we would go to their office, and I would have the PIRs printed and put in a binder to share a hard copy of each PIR with the owners. My goal for them is to stay focused on accomplishing all the PIRs as quickly as possible before my next visit to their facilities. My next visit is in two weeks for another three days. My normal schedule to be onsite with my turnaround clients is to be at their facilities Monday through Wednesday every other week.

The benefit to the owners and their company of accomplishing the PIRs is it will put money in the company's checking account by growing sales, increasing production, reducing expenses, or eliminating wasted time. My concern is that while I am away from their facilities, they will lose focus on making the changes, generating minimal progress while I am away.

It is now 6:00 a.m., and I have just enough time to finish my work, shower, and be downstairs to meet with my clients on time. At 7:50 a.m., I went downstairs to the restaurant and waited for my clients for our 8:00 meeting. Sure enough, three days out of three, they were late for our breakfast meeting by only 20 minutes. This time, Suzanne needed to explain why they were late. Since they are always late to show up for meetings, there is no good reason to offer, only another excuse. Submitting another excuse would create more embarrassment for the two of them. So now they show up, sit at the breakfast table, and be silent about why they were late.

When they finally showed up, Jonathan was all emotional while telling me that Noah and his two brothers (Peter and Mark) would be at the office at 1:00 p.m. today for a visit. Noah is the business owner from Wisconsin, whom Jonathan has been negotiating with over the past three-plus years to purchase Utah Off-road. Jonathan stated that the three brothers would visit us today primarily to meet with me to talk about Utah Off-road. Jonathan said, "Bob, I hope that you handle their visit well today because you know that the main reason we hired you was to do what you need to do to help us sell this company as soon as possible. We have been bantering with Noah about offering us a fair price to purchase our company. On my last phone call with him, Bob, Noah seemed excited about meeting you. So am I because you can get him to move on with making us a reasonable offer to purchase our business."

This surprise visit was very confusing to me. Noah and his two brothers wanting to meet with the turnaround specialist after two days at the client's facilities makes no sense to me. After two days of working here, I need more time to form an opinion about the sale price for the business. I have yet to see the financials for the company. According to Jonathan, Noah also came to meet with me and discuss my profit improvement services for his company sometime soon. Jonathan said that Noah read my three books and believes I can help his company grow in sales and profits. The meeting with Noah and his brothers was of little concern to me. My focus was to be 100% organized with the turnaround of this client.

If Noah, Peter, and Mark were genuinely interested in acquiring this company, it would be a major surprise to me. During my first two days here, I found this company to be a total mess. Whenever I have a client who wants to purchase another company, the most important asset about the target company is the quality of the management team. This company has one of the weakest management teams I have ever worked with in all my years of doing turnaround consulting. I take that back. It is not one of the weakest management teams; it is the weakest management team of any client I have worked with in 25 years. I decided to reserve my judgment concerning Noah and his family and focus completely on this client and the PIRs.

All Jonathan wanted to discuss during breakfast was Noah, Peter, and Mark and their visit today. After 15 minutes of Jonathan's non-stop dialog about the three visitors this afternoon, I tried to steer the conversation towards the PIRs. I was unsuccessful. I gave up and decided to sit there and listen to Jonathan and then focus on the PIRs when we met at the office with the list of all the PIRs in front of the two owners.

When we got to the office, it was 9:30 a.m. I asked Suzanne if I emailed her the files of the PIRs, would she please print and put two copies of each in two binders? One would be for her and the other one for Jonathan. I also asked if the three of us could meet in her office at 10:00 a.m. to get through all 15, and she nodded yes.

At 10:00 a.m. sharp, I was in Suzanne's office sitting at the conference room table, ready to start our meeting to review all the PIRs with the two owners. At 10:30, Jonathan and Suzanne walked into the office and sat at the table, ready to start the meeting. This time, Suzanne said they were late because of a domestic situation at home. I just ignored the whole situation and started the meeting. I asked Suzanne if she had the binders ready for her and Jonathan. She immediately jumped out of her chair and ran out of her office. On her way out, she said, "I will be back in five minutes." While Jonathan and I were sitting at the table waiting for her, he asked me why we were meeting this morning because he did not have much time to waste. I did not understand his question because he knew we were meeting to review the PIRs. He said he needs some time to prepare for our visitors from Wisconsin. I answered, "Jonathan, I will be 100% straight with you. As soon as Suzanne returns, this will be the most important meeting you have ever attended since you started your company. There are several topics that we are going to discuss in the next couple of hours that are going to have a positive impact on this company for many years in the future. In the first two days of my first visit to your company, I found and wrote 15 problems and issues called "PIRs" that all need fixing as soon as possible. *(See page #135.)*

Normally, it takes me three or four visits to have 15 PIRs written for a client. The problems are especially important to get fixed as quickly as possible, especially when people want to purchase your company. With Noah and his brothers visiting your facilities today, it would have been nice if we had had more advanced notice that they were traveling here for a visit. We could have had this place cleaned up and looked like a fine-tuned machine in the shop. I wish that we could have had those five vehicles in the showroom finished and looking beautiful. Jonathan, have you and Suzanne ever visited their facilities in Wisconsin?"

Jonathan answered, "Yes, we have." I asked, "Jonathan, please tell me what their facilities look like." Suzanne walked into the room with two binders and answered my question. "Bob, their facilities were gorgeous. You could eat off the floors. Their offices were beautiful and well-kept. Their shop was huge and looked brand new, but it wasn't! I could not believe how perfectly kept their facilities were in the offices, shops, and even the outside of the buildings. I am not kidding; I mean, the condition of each was over the top perfect." I asked, "Did Noah seem proud as he gave you the tour of their facilities?" Jonathan spoke up, "Bob, I didn't think so. My impression was that their facilities have been in immaculate condition since the beginning of time for their company. It impressed us because of the difference between their company and ours." All I could think about was how embarrassing the tour for Noah and his brothers of the Utah Off-road facilities would be today. I asked both owners, "Has Noah been here before?" Jonathan answered my question, "Yes, they have been here several times. Bob, I know what you are thinking. Those boys work in beautiful offices and a shop that looks state of the art. Why would they be interested in buying our company, especially in the current shape that it is in? Well, I can answer your question before you ask it. They love our products. They love how I design our offroad bumpers and other products. They would love to get into the offroad industry, and buying our company is an easy entry for them. I know that Noah believes they can manufacture our bumpers cheaper than it costs us. They buy their steel almost 30% more affordable because they buy it directly from the manufacturer. We purchase our steel from a distributor. They do enough volume with their other products that they can go now to the manufacturer, which is much less expensive, and we can't. We do not do anywhere near their volume. If they purchase our company and manufacture our products in Wisconsin, their gross profit margins will double ours.

Their powder coating operation would again lower the cost of goods compared to ours for our products. We pay retail prices to have our bumpers powder coated, and they powder coat their products. Their powder coating process is impressive. They powder coat their own products, 40% below our costs. Their operations are quality, much better than the vendor we currently use. They can build our products in one-quarter of the time it takes us with less than half the labor costs. Their shop operations are full of employees who have been there for many years with little or no employee turnover. Their company has such an amazing reputation, they have no problem recruiting people to work in their shop. If they purchased our company, their fabrication time from receiving the customer orders to shipping the products to the customer would be one week.

Utah Off-road Manufacturing
Profit Improvement Recommendation Listing
As of August 9, 20XX

#	Rating	Responsibility	PIR Description	Status
1	5	Both Owners	Dress for Success.	8/31/20XX
2	9	Jonathan	Let the buyer make the first offer if you sell your company.	12/31/20XX
3	6	Both Owners	Keep the shop, showroom, offices, etc. clean at all times.	8/31/20XX
4	8	Jonathan	Thinking out-of-the-box to improve the cashflow.	12/31/20XX
5	10	Suzanne	Seek tax advice from your tax expert.	12/31/20XX
6	10	Both Owners	Seventeen-year-old son and video games keep out of the shop.	8/7/20XX
7	10	Jonathan	Four robotic machines not operating in the shop.	8/31/20XX
8	7	Jonathan	The powder coating vendor to improve the quality of their services.	8/31/20XX
9	8	Suzanne	Research the current market salary for welders in the local area.	9/30/20XX
10	10	Jonathan	Recruit one of the adjunct instructors from WSU.	8/31/20XX
11	7	Both Owners	Meet with WSU to start an internship welding program at UOM.	12/31/20XX
12	9	Both Owners	Hire a supervisor to directly manage all shop employees.	9/30/20XX
13	5	Both Owners	Hire two labors to work in the shop to move products around.	9/30/20XX
14	7	Both Owners	Create a production incentive plan for shop employees.	9/30/20XX
15	9	Jonathan	Create installation instructions for every product sold.	9/15/20XX

We usually take six months to ship order to the customer after we receive the order. Bob, if Noah decided to start designing offroad bumpers and manufacturing them in his shop, he would put us out of business in weeks. Our only real leverage over his company is my ability to design impressive offroad bumpers. My bumper designs are the only thing right now that is keeping us in business." When Jonathan finished his speech about Noah's company, Suzanne was frustrated hearing what he said because she knew it was all true and embarrassing.

The fact that Jonathan and Suzanne have hired me to improve their company's performance, cash flow, and profits will be the opposite of what Noah wants to happen to this company. My turnaround efforts are going to delay him from buying this company. When I finish this consulting engagement, it will materially increase the potential purchase price of Utah Off-road that Noah would have to pay. Noah and his brothers are going to pump me for information. I must be careful with what I say or do anything that will hurt my clients, Suzanne and Jonathan.

I asked the owners, "Have you shared your financial statements with Noah?" Suzanne answered, "Yes, we have. Those three guys visiting us today know everything there is to know about this company." I continued, "Well then, we have nothing to hide from them, but let me give you some advice for the future. Never do you let anyone peek under your skirt. In other words, see the company's financial statements before they have (1) signed a nondisclosure agreement, (2) proved to you that they have the funds to purchase the company, and (3) have some skin in the game, meaning put down a deposit against the purchase price. Only when you satisfy those three things do you let anyone do any due diligence on your company!"

I could tell that Jonathan was getting irritated with my comments because I was explaining how he screwed up his business dealings with Noah. I decided I could not buffer my words, or he would not learn anything while I was here. I'm here to help him, his wife, and his company to grow in sales, cash flow, and profits.

I looked at Suzanne and said, "Are you ready to go over the PIRs now?" Jonathan said, "Bob, can we postpone this meeting until later this afternoon? I want to review all your work here and write down any questions I may have before we go over these PRIs." I answered, "Jonathan, that is fine with me, but they are PIRs (Profit Improvement Recommendations), not PRIs." Jonathan said, "Okay, Bob, I get it! We can discuss this as soon as the three brothers leave."

With a raised level of emotion, I said, "My good friend, these Profit Improvement Recommendations will save your company. These PIRs will make your company salable to a buyer for a much better price than today's value. These PIRs will change your business's purchase price from receiving a "bottom-feeder" sales price offer to one that could make you a rich man. Your attitude sucks and is offensive. You have had a close-up view of what I did to your friend's company less than a year ago. I turned it around, and now he is a rich man rather than worrying about having enough cash to make payroll every two weeks. After I finish my work, let me tell you the difference between your company then and your company now. It is quite simple; it is likely between $4,000,000 and $6,000,000 more in your pocket after selling the company. Consider the difference in your life, your wife's, and your children's lives with an additional $5,000,000 in your checking account."

Jonathan, you hired me, and I am doing a job to do the same thing with comparable results as I did with Brian's company, ABC Off-road Distributors." Jonathan said, "Bob, what are you saying? I don't understand the problem!" "There is no problem. If we have enough time to review each PIR today, go over each action plan, and you and your wife commit that you will work on accomplishing each PIR between now and my next visit, I do not have a problem! I want to explain something. You and Suzanne want to sell this business. I aim to help you sell it to the right person at the maximum sale price. Think about this! Assume the company does $7,000,000 to $8,000,000 in sales and $1,000,000 in profits in the next 12 months. What would be the difference in the sales price compared to the business's results today? I will answer the question for you. The sales price would be millions of dollars less. With the status of the company right now, only a "bottom-feeder" would buy your company. The buyer would try to steal the company from you for a minimal amount. Their next step is cleaning up the company just like you hired me to do. Then, they would resell the business to another buyer. The only difference would be that the sales price would be two or three times the sale price that they purchased the company from you and Suzanne."

"I hate to tell you, but my impression of why you and Noah have not had a sales transaction together yet is because he is waiting for you to get in financial and cash flow trouble. He will bail you out for the minimum sales offer when you are in trouble."

"Bob, we are not doing that bad. Have you reviewed our financials yet?" "No sir, I have not. But let me share my feelings about your financial statement and current cash situation. Under these current conditions, you sell your bumpers to the customers, and the customers pay 100% of the product's sale price. You do not deliver the customer's product for six months, meaning you have their money in your checking account for five months without having any cost for the product. If this company did not have all the customer's money upfront for five months' worth of customer orders, you would have cash flow problems. Because you have been using customer deposits for five months, you are hiding your cash flow problems. You use your company's customer deposits as a bank line of credit. Do you think if you were not using the customer deposit as operating cash, would the company even be able to make your weekly payroll deposit?" Jonathan gave me a serious look and responded, "Bob, I will prioritize reading and analyzing each of your PIRs. I will be ready for our meeting today after Noah and his brothers leave. Are there any PIRs that are the most important that I should focus on?"

"Yes." I responded, "The first 15!" Jonathan looked at the first page in the binder, which is a recap of each PIR, and said, "Bob, there are only 15 PIRs in my binder." With a frustrated look, I said, "Jonathan, every one of these PIRs is important. You will notice a one to ten rating on the recap for each PIR. The ones rated with an eight, nine, or ten are the PIRs that are the most important to focus on first. Those PIRs have the biggest cash flow and budgetary impact on the company once you accomplish all the action steps. But let me make this clear: Every PIR is important. The eights, nines, and tens are the highest priority to start on immediately. It is important for the two of you to completely understand each PIR and have a game plan on how to attack each one. The overall goal is to do everything we can to increase production, maintain the quality of the products, and get the customer backlog report down to two or three weeks. There are several PIRs in your binder to accomplish with little or no cash outlay, but they will improve the business's cash flow. For example, we can hire a computer programmer to program the four robotic welders and grinders; that action will not cost this company anything. As you know, the company you purchased the four pieces of equipment from said they would reimburse you for all the costs for a programmer to get those four machines up and working properly. If these pieces of equipment were working, the production of this shop would materially increase immediately. When the production increases, so does that cash flow!" With a stern look, Jonathan asked, "Bob, are you blaming me for those four pieces of equipment not working?" "No sir, I am not. I did not write the PIRs to blame anyone. They are all written to make changes to this operation to:

1. Increase production,

2. Maintain the quality of the products,

3. Improve the safety conditions in the shop,

4. Improve the appearance of the showroom,

5. Improve the quality of the powder coating vendor,

6. Ship two to four times the number of bumpers to the customers weekly, and

7. Ship all the customer orders with the installation instructions so the customer can install their bumper if they choose to."

"Okay, Bob, I understand your message; I will be ready for our PIR meeting this afternoon."

*   *   *

I spent the rest of the morning sitting at the conference room table in Suzanne's office, reviewing the financial statements for my client's business. Suzanne had emailed me the prior three years plus the first six months of the current year's income statement and balance sheets for the same period. At exactly 1:00 p.m., Jonathan and Suzanne walked into the office with three gentlemen following them. I immediately stood up, and Jonathan said, "Bob Curry, I would like to introduce you to three of my very good friends from Wisconsin, Noah, Peter, and Mark."

Noah was a handsome gentleman with a very friendly smile. Noah is six foot tall and 235 lbs. He looked like a big, ole, nice guy! His smile could melt butter while it was still in the refrigerator. He was wearing his company's logoed dress shirt and khakis, as were Peter and Mark. They all looked very professional. I hate to say this, but they all looked much more professional than my two clients, Jonathan and Suzanne. When I saw these three gentlemen, I started thinking that I hoped their professional appearance would rub off on my two clients, which was the subject of my first PIR, Dress for Success. I had little faith that their professionalism would rub off on Jonathan and Suzanne. There was no problem telling that they were all brothers with a couple of years of age differences. All three of them had that same warm smile. They all had exceptionally light complexions that come with living in Wisconsin. There are no beaches to tan in Wisconsin like in Fort Lauderdale, Florida.

Noah reached out his right hand to shake hands, as did I. When we shook hands, he gently pulled me closer and asked, "Bob, I don't know if Jonathan told you, but I am a big fan of yours." He was carrying a briefcase and sat it on the conference room table. He opened it and grabbed a copy of my three books. All three of the books looked like they were all well-read because there were a bunch of the corners of pages folded over to mark his place in the book as he read it. He handed them to me and asked, "Could you please autograph my copy of your books?" Noah was acting like a little kid. It was like he was asking Michael Jordan to autograph a "MJ" Chicago Bulls Jersey for him. I was surprised and flattered when Noah asked me to sign my books the first minute we met. He said, "I am a huge fan of yours. I have read all three of your books and learned much about business from your writings! We are using many of the forms and reports that you exhibited in your books in our companies. My favorite is the "Weekly Flash Report" that I receive from our controller every Monday by 3:00 p.m. When I review that weekly report, I know exactly my company's financial status, and it only takes me five minutes to analyze and understand the numbers." (*See the Weekly Flash Report and Instructions on pages #154 to #159.*)

Noah seemed like the type of person who could become your best friend in the first 15 minutes we met. Peter and Mark stepped around Noah, and Mark said, "Bob, please excuse Noah. He has no manners. Let me introduce myself and my younger brother. I am Mark, and that's Peter." It was quite easy to tell that Noah was the oldest brother and the leader of the family and company. He just had that leadership personality.

I sat at the table, signed all three books, and returned them to Noah. He put the books back into his briefcase, closed it, put the briefcase on the floor, and then sat down at the table. He asked Jonathan, "Are we going to meet now, or do you have something else planned?" Jonathan responded, "Yes, let's meet now. We did not have a formal itinerary for your visit today. I assumed that the three of you would like to talk more about the operations of Utah Off-road, especially since Bob is here doing his profit improvement magic. Noah, did the three of you have a specific agenda that you wanted to accomplish today?" Noah said, "Well, we planned to come down here in September, but when we heard that you hired Bob, we moved our plans up for the visit to this week. Peter and Mark have been looking at land and warehouse space in this area for us to buy or lease. So, during this visit, three of us will check out what they found." Suzanne went over to the mini refrigerator in the corner of the room and asked the group, "Who all wants a bottle of water?" Everyone indicated that they wanted one and sat down at the table. Suzanne passed out the water and then sat at the table with a tablet for her to take notes.

Noah started the conversation, "So Bob, what are you doing here for Jonathan's and Suzanne's company?" My first thought was to be careful with my answers to Noah's questions. "Noah, as you know from reading my books, I am a business consultant. Clients hire me to improve the financial performance of their businesses. Jonathan's good friend has a company about ten miles down the road that I worked with about a year ago. Brian is a different man now than he was two years ago. His stress level today is much lower. Improving his company's financial performance changed Brian's life. I plan to do the same for this company and its two owners! Can you imagine what Jonathan would be like without the stress of this business? No? All kidding aside, these two owners have a great company, and I am here to do some cleanup and profit improvement."

"If I were younger, I would give these two owners an offer to buy their business if they would sell it to me. My wife was President of City College in Florida. We just sold the college so we could both move on to retirement. If I told my wife I was interested in buying a business in Utah, she would never speak to me again!" Noah asked, "Bob, are you serious? Do you like this business so much that you would consider buying the company from Jonathan and Suzanne? This company is only doing $3,200,000 a year. What do you think is its potential?" Noah's questions started, and I knew I had to be careful with my answers. "Noah, much like Brian's business down the road, this business has a huge upside also. Brian's business has more than doubled its sales in the past 12 months, and this company has a much bigger upside than Brian's business. Some years ago, I took over a computer distributor company in Pennsylvania and grew the sales of that company from $48,000,000 to $130,000,000 in nine months. I am sure you recognize the story because that turnaround is the story in my second book, "The Turnaround." This company has a huge upside of growing sales and profits. I have only been here for two days, and from what I have seen, I have great confidence that I could do the same sales and profit growth here in a few months." Mark asked, "Bob, that is interesting to us. How are you going to do that for this business?" I paused and answered, "Mark, I do not have permission to talk to anyone about my client's business. And to be very honest, I have only been here since Monday. My limited knowledge of this business is due to two days of consulting. But I have enough information about the offroad industry and this company's quality products to speak confidently. Their products are one of the leaders in the industry. As I am sure you know, my prior client was a distributor of offroad products. Brian has huge respect for Jonathan's designs of the front and back bumpers for offroad vehicles. I trust Brian. He knows the offroad industry like no one I have ever met." Jonathan said, "I agree with you, Bob. Brian knows his stuff about aftermarket offroad products!" He told me there is a huge upside for this business. With my brief period here, I agree with his opinion."

There was a long pause in the conversation. I looked at Jonathan and Suzanne; they were smiling as they listened to the conversation and enjoyed every word. I was saying all the right things as per their wishes. I was trying to sell this company to the company owned and managed by these three gentlemen. Before the three brothers asked another question, I said, "Noah, I know you and Jonathan have had conversations about your company buying this business. I am a hired consultant working for the owners of this business. I must be careful with what I tell you about the business until you have signed a nondisclosure agreement with this company."

"Bob," said Noah, "You don't understand our relationship between me, my brothers, Jonathan, and Suzanne! We are all friends and have been for many years. You don't need to be secretive about this business. We are here today, just visiting our friends!" I asked, "So, Noah, help me understand, you are or are not interested in buying this company?" Noah answered, "Of course we are. We would love to own their business. But don't get me wrong, these are our friends!" I responded to

Noah's comment, "Noah, I am so sorry. I hope that I did not offend you with my comments!" "Hmm... no problem, Bob. I do have a list of questions that we would love to get your opinion on these topics about this business." Noah pulled a tablet out of his briefcase and handed it to me. There was a handwritten list of 17 questions. I took a minute and read all the questions and gave the list to Jonathan to see. Jonathan read the list and handed it back to me. Jonathan looked at me and slightly nodded his head, 'Yes.'

I looked across the table at Noah, Peter, and Mark, then asked, "Do you mind if I answer your questions not in the same order they are written?" Noah shook his head and said, "Bob, that's not a problem." I looked back at the list after a long hesitation and said, "Yes, no, yes, no, yes, soon, no, I think so, possibly, I doubt it, yes, no, several times, I don't have enough information yet to answer that question, that is your responsibility, yes, and of course." Mark said, "Bob, you are a funny guy! Is this your way of saying you will not answer our questions about this company?" I answered, "Not yet! You know we need to get some paperwork signed to protect my client before I answer any questions. Also, today is my third day here at Utah Off-road. I am good at what I do for a living, but I am not an expert on the topic of Jonathan's and Suzanne's company yet. If you have a sincere interest in having this conversation with me, come back in a month, and I will be able to have a good working knowledge of the details of this company. Mark looked at Noah and said, "See, I told you that it was too early to come down here and pump Bob for information about this business!" Mark surprised me when he said that in front of Jonathan, Suzanne, and me!

Noah looked at me and said, "Bob, please excuse my brother Mark for his comments. He is young and still makes a lot of mistakes. We drove from Wisconsin to Utah to meet you and see if you would be interested in coming to our company in Wisconsin. We would like you to do the same thing for us that you are doing here for Jonathan and Suzanne and did very well for Brian and his partner, Jordan. We are a profitable company, but we can do so much better. When I read your three books, as I said before, I became a huge fan of yours. When Jonathan hired you, it freaked me out. It felt weird that Jonathan hired the author of the three books I read. As soon as I talked to Jonathan and he said that you would be here this week, I wanted to come and meet you to see if you had time available to visit us. I told my brothers about my idea about you coming to our company for profit improvement consulting. Mark suggested we also ask you questions about Utah Off-road while we meet here today."

I answered, "Noah, I appreciate the offer. It is very flattering for you and your brothers to come to Utah for us to meet, and you offer me a consulting engagement with your company. As you know, I am under contract with this company, and there would be an absolute conflict of interest if I represented both of your companies. The only way I could work for you is if you each signed an agreement to hire me as a consultant, and neither of you could sue me. I would work for each company, helping you make more money with your respective businesses. If I gave you my opinion on the valuation of Jonathan's and Suzanne's business, I would base it on my analysis of the status of their business and my thoughts about how much we could grow its sales, cash flow, and profits. Because you are all friends already, the possible conflict of interest would be less of a problem. If all five of you are interested in me working for the two entities, you must decide and let me know once you have talked."

Noah said, "Bob, we don't need to talk. We did that already. The five of us have already agreed that you can consult with both companies, and it will not be a problem for any of us. If you do for all of us what you did for Brian and Jordan and the other companies in your other two books, we all would be proud to have you on our team. We have decided that having you consult for both companies would be a win–win situation for everyone, including you!"

I was shocked. I did not expect this. I told the five owners that I would have my attorney draft a waiver for any conflict of interest and have it in your hands before the weekend. "Noah, I will need you to send me the email addresses for the three of you today. I will draft a consulting agreement in my hotel room tonight and email it to you later. If you and your brothers read and agree with the terms and conditions, please sign and return it to me. The contract will contain the same terms and conditions Jonathan and Suzanne recently signed. I am flying home tomorrow morning. I will sign the contract tomorrow when I get home and email you a completely executed copy of the agreement for your files. After we have a signed contract, I will review my schedule and let you know when I can visit your facilities during the next two months."

All five owners stood up, and I shook hands with each person. Noah said, "Bob, I look forward to you visiting our facilities and meeting our management team. I plan to purchase copies of your three books for the management team. I am going to ask them to read them before you visit us. They will all learn a lot about business and improve their performance for our company. Most of our managers have worked for the company for many years. They only know how to manage their area of responsibility by doing everything "our way" of doing things. I want them all to open their minds and think about doing everything better, more efficiently, and more profitable. I want them all to grow in their respective jobs. Unfortunately, that will not happen if I am the only one telling them how to do things. I want a fresh pair of eyes to see our operations and suggest how we can upgrade our processes, our reporting, and how we manage our people. We are doing many good things, but I don't think "good" is good enough! I want our company to be great! Bob, when I read your first book, I decided that you are the guy to do this for us. Then, when I read your other two books, I knew that you were the perfect person to help us upgrade our team and how we currently manage our business."

I walked around the conference room table to shake Noah's hand. Peter and Mark stepped closer, and I shook both of their hands. I immediately had a good feeling about these three guys. The meeting continued for another hour, and then the three brothers left to look at some land and warehouses to either lease or purchase. They did not reveal what they would use the local property or warehouse space for.

*　　*　　*

Immediately after our meeting ended, Jonathan said that he and Suzanne would be ready to discuss the list of PIRs in 15 minutes. I asked Jonathan what he thought about today's meeting with Noah and his brothers. Jonathan said that it went extremely well. He continued, "Bob, I know that they do not trust me because of the status of our company right now. The shop and showroom are a mess. Noah is a perfectionist; our business would not please a perfectionist's eye. He respects your skills and ability to whip our business into shape, and then he will be ready to sit down at the table and start negotiating to buy our company." I replied, "Young man, I hope you are right!"

At 3:00 p.m., Jonathan and Suzanne walked into her office together, sat at the table, and opened their binders. Jonathan said, "Bob, I have read every word of the 15 PIRs. Everything that you wrote makes a great deal of business sense. You have written the PIRs professionally and comprehensively. I only have one question to ask concerning your work. Where will we get the money to make the payroll for all the employees you want to add to your plan?" I responded, "Jonathan, that is quite easy to answer! When this company starts receiving customer orders, manufacturing the products, and shipping them to the customers in 2 to 3 weeks, your sales will instantly grow by 200% to 300% compared to the last 12 months. You are losing a ton of sales because you cannot manufacture and ship the products in a reasonable time."

"This company has a terrible reputation in the offroad industry because it takes the customers six months to receive the products they ordered. Your friend Brian will not order any products from you because he does not want your company to give his business a bad reputation because of how long it takes you to ship your customer orders. He told me himself if he bought your bumpers for his customers, all his customers would get mad at him." He said, "If I order bumpers from Jonathan and get them in six months, my customers will be mad at me for taking so long. I can use a different vendor, receive the order in two weeks, install them, and make a profit!"

I continued, "Jonathan, Brian is not the only distributor that feels that way about your company. They all do! No offroad distributor can make any money dealing with your company. Not only can they not make any money, but they also will get their customers mad at their company to the point that they will stop buying from that distributor. Your slow production times are hurting all the distributors in your industry if they buy their products from your company. There are only a few distributors in the USA who are buying products from your company, hurting your business."

I asked, "So, now that you both have read the PIRs and understand them, my first question is, do you agree with them? Do you think they will all help your business grow and be more profitable?" Both owners shook their heads. 'Yes.' "Well then, please give me an idea as to which ones you will start to focus on." Jonathan started, "We should get a computer programmer in here first and get those robotic welders and grinders working. We should visit Weber State and build relationships with the welding program instructors. Second, I plan to meet the owner of our powder coating vendor this Friday to show him how poorly the quality of his powder coating is coming from his company. Between all those meetings, I will finish installing the bumpers on the vehicles in the showroom. In the evenings, rather than playing video games with my son, I will develop a list of all the products we sell that need installation instructions. Then, I will work on writing them until we have instructions for every product we sell." Suzanne said, "Bob, I plan first to clean up this showroom, the offices, and the bathrooms so they are presentable to any visitor in the future. I will talk to a recruiter in the area and search for an accounting manager or a controller to upgrade our accounting department and its reporting. I will also talk to the recruiter about hiring a shop supervisor who is a certified welder."

With a big smile, I said, "I am proud of the two of you. You understand how important it is to make these changes to your company to improve sales, cash flow, and profits. Under the business's current conditions, Noah and his two brothers will never purchase your company. It would be best if you focused as much time as possible to accomplish each PIR. The only way you will sell this business at the true market price is to focus on the PIRs. When you open these binders, and every one of the Action Plans is complete, you will be ready to sell." There is no doubt that the two of you will have to work your tails off both managing this business and working on accomplishing all the PIRs!" Suzanne asked, "Bob, based on your prior experiences, how long do you think it will take us to make all these changes in our binders?" "Suzanne, I can give you an accurate answer to your question. I was at ABC Off-road Supply for seven months. But that company is much bigger than your business, with about three or four times that number of employees. All your sales come from your website, so I don't have to worry about upgrading your sales team like I did for Brian and Jordan. I would estimate I should finish all my work here by year-end."

Suzanne told Jonathan, "Remind me when we go home tonight to tell the kids that we will see them next January because we will be here at the office working on Bob's list! We also need to tell them to get ready to answer the front door to get their dinner from the "*Door Dash*" drivers!" Jonathan responded, "But if we can get this place cleaned up and sold at the number I want for the business, think about the beautiful home we can buy mortgage-free!"

I finished the conversation with, "What I did not tell you is that I have not yet reviewed your financial statements, tax returns, website, and marketing. I have focused my first week on reviewing your shop operations. So, have it in your mind that these 15 PIRs are just the beginning of my work for this company." Jonathan said that he was glad that I was going home tomorrow. The 15 PIRs are enough for us to get depressed! He was smiling as he was making his laughable comment. Suzanne said that she was leaving in the next ten minutes. She asked me if I needed a ride to the hotel. I said that I would be ready in five minutes. I have a consulting agreement to draft tonight for Noah and his brothers.

I showered and changed into casual clothes when I returned to my hotel room. I went downstairs to get some dinner. I wanted to have a vodka and tonic, but instead, I had two cups of coffee because I had a consulting agreement to write and email to possible new clients, Noah, Mark, and Peter.

Company Name
Weekly Flash Report
for Week Ending 08/15/20XX

Cash Activity	
Beginning Balance	
Plus: Receipts	
Cash Available	
Less:	
A/P Disbursements	
P/R Disbursements	
Ending Balance	

Loan Activity	
Beginning balance (last week)	
Plus: New borrowings	
Less: Amount paid down	
Plus: Interest and fees	
Ending Balance for this week	

Accounts Receivable Aging

	Last Week $	%	Two Weeks Ago $	%	Three Weeks Ago $	%	Four weeks Ago $	%
Current								
31 – 60 days (past due)								
61 – 90 days (past due)								
Over 90 days (past due)								
Grand Total								

Accounts Payable Aging

	Last Week $	%	Two Weeks Ago $	%	Three Weeks Ago $	%	Four weeks Ago $	%
Current								
31 – 60 days (past due)								
61 – 90 days (past due)								
Over 90 days (past due)								
Grand Total								

Payroll Summary

	Last Week $	#	Two Weeks Ago $	#	Three Weeks Ago $	#	Four weeks Ago $	#
Production Labor								
S, G & A Labor								
Grand Total								

Sales Summary

	Last Week $	#	Two Weeks Ago $	#	Three Weeks Ago $	#	Four weeks Ago $	#
Jobs Installed								
Service Billed								
Quotes Prepared								
New Contracts								
Backlog status								

Weekly Flash Report Instructions

Goals of Flash Reporting

Preparing the Weekly Flash Report is from essential business indicator information in the various financial and operating reports. The controller is responsible for the overall coordination and preparation, but the management team provides all the data.

The Goals of the Flash Report are the following:

1. Provide senior management with a current "snapshot" of the previous week's key business indicator statistics.

2. Allow management to become initiative-taking in reacting to changes in trends or areas needing attention.

3. Establish a common ground for management focus to help achieve predetermined operating performance and financial results.

Preparing this report requires participation from the sales and marketing, operational, and financial functional areas to measure and monitor vital operating statistics weekly rather than only the monthly/quarterly financial statements.

Benefits of Weekly Flash Reporting

The benefits of the Weekly Flash Report are the following:

1. Focusing senior management on key business indicator

statistics by functional area of the company (sales and marketing, operations, financial, etc.) rather than an infrequent review of the company in total.

2. Setting and monitoring goals weekly to achieve preferred results.

3. The weekly reporting of this report creates an initiative-taking, instead of reactive, management style.

4. Initiating communication between senior management of all functional areas and focused attention on the company's common goals and objectives.

5. Giving each manager a view of the company's performance—successes or problem areas that should receive attention immediately.

6. Helping to eliminate confusion and misinterpretation of the company's most current results of operations.

Weekly Flash Report Procedure

Reporting Frequency

Preparing the Weekly Flash Report *(See page #154)* will highlight the company's weekly financial and operational results. The report is ready immediately after the weekly payroll report is final for the prior week, Monday through Saturday. The development of the report template format is on Microsoft Excel. Senior management can revise it and adjust the data to their customized needs.

The report will contain information for the most current week ending and the prior three weeks, providing one month of history.

Information Included

The report contains six sections of information: Cash Activity, Line of Credit, Accounts Receivable Aging, Accounts Payable Aging, Company Payroll (both dollars and headcount), Sales Trends, and any other information that senior management desires.

The information reported is as follows:

Cash Activity

The cash data is a recap of the week's cash activity. You are classifying the disbursements into three types: Accounts Payable Disbursements (A/P Disbursements), Payroll Disbursements (P/R Disbursements), and Debt Service. This report reflects the actual cash activity, and you should remember the exact information included in the Eight-Week Cash Forecast actual column for the prior week.

Line of Credit Activity

The line of credit data for the week's activity should include the following:

1. The Borrowing Base Calculation: The amount of borrowing

available based on the assets required by the bank to collateralize the loan.

2. The Current Line Usage: The total amount of money borrowed by the company as of the date of report preparation.

3. Line Available: The subtraction of the Current Line Usage from the Borrowing Base.

4. Percentage Used: The percentage of the line of credit used.

5. Current borrowing interest rate.

Accounts Receivable Activity

The report contains four weeks of accounts receivable aging information (current, 1 to 29 days, 30 days to 59, 60 to 89 days, and over 90 days), both dollars and percentages.

Accounts Payable Activity

Four weeks of accounts payable aging information (current, 1 to 29 days, 30 days to 59, 60 to 89 days, and over 90 days) are reported in both dollars and percentages.

Company Payroll Activity

They divide four weeks of gross payroll information into the production, selling, general, and administrative departments. They are reporting this information in dollars and by headcount by category.

Sales Trends

They report four weeks of sales data, all obtained from the billing records and the estimating system. The information is the following:

1. Jobs Shipped

2. Jobs Billed

3. Quotes Prepared

4. Customer Orders Received

5. Current backlog Status

Responsibilities

The controller/accounting manager is responsible for preparing the flash report.

Distribution

The report should be distributed to the Management Committee by 3:00 p.m. each Monday.

Conclusion

Reporting weekly information to the company management team will provide them with tools for quick and immediate decision-making, allowing each manager to keep their finger on the pulse of their respective departments.

Chapter 7

A BLACK LONG SLEEVE LOGOED SHIRT AND KHAKIS

"Great things in business are never done by one person. They're done by a team of people."
— STEVE JOBS – AN AMERICAN BUSINESS MAGNATE, AND INVENTOR. HE WAS THE CO-FOUNDER, CHAIRMAN, & CEO OF APPLE.

Monday, August 22nd – Day 4 of week 2 of the turnaround engagement

I FLEW INTO SALT LAKE CITY AIRPORT ON SUNDAY night and took an Uber to my hotel. I woke up early and reviowod all my filcs for Utah Off-road. At 7.50 a.m., I was In the hotel restaurant with a hot coffee, ready to meet my two clients for breakfast. At 7:55, Jonathan and Suzanne walked into the restaurant for our 8:00 breakfast meeting and sat at my table. I was surprised they were on time for the meeting, but I did not say anything.

The shocking surprise was when I saw what they were wearing. Jonathan wore a black long-sleeved business shirt with the company's logo on the pocket. He was wearing a pair of khakis with a new pair of work boots. Suzanne wore the same black logoed shirt with black jeans and loafers. They both looked 100% different, different meaning better than they looked two weeks ago. What a vast improvement compared to my last trip. This accomplishment may be a good sign that the owners would have a great report to talk about regarding the list of PIRs for their company.

They sat down at the table after we shook hands. Suzanne said, "Welcome back to Utah, Bob. We were both looking forward to your visit this week! You will be surprised when you see all the changes to the office. We have worked hard for the past ten days, which has been gratifying." I smiled and said, "I am so excited; tell me about what has happened since my last visit." It was Jonathan's turn to talk, "Bob, when we went home on your last day here, we had dinner with the family. After dinner, Suzanne and I sat at our kitchen table with our PIRs binders and developed a plan. We knew that we could not accomplish every one of the action steps by ourselves, so we decided to delegate some of the tasks to our employees. It worked out well."

Our waitress approached our table and asked if we wanted to order breakfast. Each of us ordered an omelet, bacon, and wheat toast. Jonathan ordered orange juice, Suzanne ordered a glass of iced water, and I asked the waitress to warm up my coffee when she returned with the food.

"We offered all the shop employees extra hours if they wanted to work after their shift. They all accepted the offer. The first thing that they accomplished was to finish putting together the five vehicles in the showroom. It took five guys two evenings to install the bumpers and winches with my help.

We moved all the vehicles to one side of the showroom, and the team cleaned up the empty half.

We hired a cleaning company to scrub and wax the floor. I hired the cleaning company because I decided waxing floors differed from our expertise. Our shop staff could help us make other improvements to the showroom which would be a better use of their time. I could not believe how beautiful the floor looked after they finished the job. After they finished the first half, we moved everything to the other side, and they cleaned and waxed the rest of the showroom. We pulled everything off the walls and hung current advertising posters for many vendors. After we finish everything on our list, we will invite our vendors into our showroom for a visit. We hired a company to detail the five vehicles. They did a beautiful job washing and waxing the vehicles, making them all look beautiful. We lined them all up on the right side of the room, the perfect distance apart from each other. Now, you can enter any of them without the car doors bumping into the car parked next to it. We took pictures of each vehicle to post the photographs on our website and social media. I had taken pictures of each vehicle before dismantling the original bumpers. The "before and after" pictures look great on our website. I am sure our customers appreciated seeing the pictures and the changes made to the vehicles. We have already received several orders from posting those pictures.

We also contacted the Jeep, Ford, and Lexus dealerships in the area and sold the original bumpers I removed from the five vehicles. That deal worked out great for us. The extra money we made from that deal and the new bumper orders we received from the posted pictures paid for the additional payroll dollars for the shop employees."

"After cleaning and rearranging the showroom with the five vehicles on the right side, the rest looked empty. We had six old Jeeps and Broncos in a storage garage that we used to take to the offroad shows to display at our booth. We had the detailing service we hired for the vehicles in the showroom wash and waxed those cars. We put them in the showroom. Once the room was clean, I wished we had done this years ago. Bob, you will not believe the difference in the room now compared to two weeks ago. We plan to post pictures of those old cars on our website and sell them off individually. After we sell one, we will replace it with another vehicle from one of the dealerships. Only this time, we will not buy jeeps, SUVs, or pickup trucks!

After we install our offroad products on new vehicles, we will put them in our showroom until we return them to the dealers. The goal is to be able to sell cars to our dealership customers with our offroad products already installed. I have made appointments with the local Ford, Lexus, Jeep, and Toyota dealerships to talk about our shop installing offroad bumpers on a couple of their vehicles for their showroom. I have already met with the dealership's Jeep and Lexus general managers, and they loved the idea. Bob, I showed up to talk to the GM wearing my new work outfit and got some positive reactions. I have known these guys for years. They have seen me dressed like I have worked in the shop as a welder for many years. It gave me a wonderful feeling with all the positive comments."

The waitress brought our food and drinks. The omelets looked great. I did not eat dinner last night, so I was hungry. I was looking forward to putting the napkin on my lap and eating breakfast. Our conversation stopped for the first 15 minutes after we all started eating.

Jonathan continued talking about his and his wife's past ten days, "Suzanne and the ladies who work in the office cleaned their offices and bathrooms. We hired a cleaning service to visit the offices weekly to keep the showroom, offices, and bathrooms in the same condition. After the offices and bathroom were all cleaned up and looking great, I wished we had tried long ago to keep the facilities looking like they do now. One important thing that Suzanne and I learned from this cleaning project is that our employees have come up large. They all showed us that they care about Suzanne and the company! Unfortunately, they still think that I am the crazy guy in the office." Suzanne said, "Bob, you know that Jonathan is just kidding. Our employees love my husband, plus they respect him for his designs of our offroad products. But there are times that I do think that he is whacky!" Jonathan said, "She is right; I agree; I get whacky when stressed. My stress level has dropped since we have accomplished many of the action items in our PIRs binders. I had no idea it would be easy to get this stuff done when we used our employees to help with each project. Now that we have kicked butt with some tasks, it is much easier to plan for the list of other stuff we need to accomplish."

"Last Monday, my friend, who owns the powder coating company we use, located right across the street from our shop, came to our offices to meet. I had our employee (Jake), who delivers the bumpers to their facilities and picks them up, sit in the meeting. Thank goodness Jake recorded how many rejected bumpers there were during the past month. Jake also took pictures of the rejected bumpers with the bad powder coating jobs. He also kept statistics on how long it took them to powder coat a bumper. The statistics made both him and me sick when we reviewed the numbers.

Because of the poor powder coating quality, the rejected bumpers were at 22% rejections, which was terrible. The average bumper delivered to their shop took ten days, which could have been better. The three of us all reviewed the numbers, and my friend was disgusted with the results of his staff. I understood his feelings because I was equally, if not more, unhappy with the results. My friend offered us, in compensation for their inferior quality of service, his company would powder coat all the bumpers that we currently have at his shop, plus the next two weeks of our deliveries for free. He said he would stay here locally for at least the next two months to clean up the powder coating operations. He apologized for their terrible quality. He assured me that the powder coating quality and the bumpers' turnaround time would improve immediately. I asked him to please send me his offer in writing. I appreciated his offering not to bill us for the existing products at his shop, plus the next two weeks' deliveries. He assured me that I would have that agreement in writing before the day ended.

I knew he would clean up our powder coating problems within two weeks. I knew he wanted to sell his business, and he could not do that with operations as bad as they were. My employee, Jake, who attended the meeting, learned a lot and thanked me for letting him be there. He told me that he felt handcuffed and that their powder coating sucked, and he did not know what to do about it.

I felt bad because Jake and the rest of the employees in the shop should have felt comfortable coming to me to help resolve the problems. Jonathan looked at me and said, "Bob, I must look at myself in the mirror. I know that I have a problem and that my staff does not have the confidence to come to me to help them solve the company's shop problems.

Because of this meeting, I have learned that all employees need a supervisor to oversee their work, or their production will suffer. The owner of the powder coating company tried to move to Arizona and still manage his company, but he failed. Absentee ownership or absentee supervision of the company does not work!" I responded, "Jonathan, just hearing you say that tells me that you are growing to be a better manager and owner of this company. Neither you nor your wife have formal training in running a business. I hope that during this engagement, you both learn more about managing your company profitably." With a spirited tone, Jonathan said, "Bob, believe me, Suzanne and I have learned a lot, and this is only your fourth day here." I asked Jonathan, "Are there any other stories you have to share about the past two weeks?"

Jonathan said, "Yes, Bob, we hired a part-time computer programmer to work on getting the two robotic welders and grinders working. He is an adjunct instructor at Weber State. The instructor started working on Friday morning and was in the shop most of the weekend. I know that he has one of the two robotic welders working already. I just realized those welders work well when repeatedly doing the same welding project. But, when you have all the varied sizes and shapes of bumpers or any of our other products, they all require programming individually. Then, if you are going to weld the same bumper a week later, you must call up that program, and it will do the job again automatically. So, what is taking so long to do the programming?"

We have many assorted bumper designs for all the other models and years of vehicles. We program each bumper to the machine's computer and then that program to the inventory of programs. So, if we have one hundred different models of bumpers, all one hundred need programming and then added to the list of programs. Bob, if I had known this, I would never have purchased these machines. I checked our current backlog of orders for customers. We have sold 95% of the bumper models on our list of products. We can sort all the different models in the backlog report. Then, we can weld all those bumpers first on the programmed welder and grinder for the models we have sold the most. While fabricating those bumpers, the instructor is programming the second machine for the other models. He has about 20 models programmed on the one welder and grinder. The finished programs on the welder are the same programs for the grinders. As he is programming the second two machines, he can work on welding and grinding orders faster than two or three of our existing welders. This additional production will reduce our customer backlog from six to two months in the next 30 days."

"And also, I called the company that I purchased the four machines. I told them that, as per their offer to pay for the cost of a computer programmer, I had hired a programmer and his assistant. I am paying the programmer $50 per hour and the assistant $40 per hour. I emailed the company and attached an invoice for 40 hours per week for both programmers for four weeks of programming. The company wired us $14,400 in advance to pay for the programmer and his assistant. The day we received that money in our checking account was another wonderful day at Utah Off-road." With a confused look, I asked, "Jonathan, did you hire an assistant programmer?" He answered, "No, Bob, one of my welders in the shop will oversee all the programming in the future. He works with the programmer every minute he is in the shop. He is training in computer programming for the two welders and grinders. We need a backup programmer if the adjunct instructor is no longer interested in working for us. The backup programmer is just an insurance policy to ensure we always have a programming resource at the company."

I was impressed with Jonathan's actions. It was brilliant to contact and pre-bill the equipment company, so his company was within the budget to pay for the programmer. I asked Jonathan, "Have you got the programmer's estimate of how long he believes it will take to do all the programming for those machines?" Jonathan replied, "Yes, I have! He said, worst case that it would take another two weeks to get all the work done. The good news is that he said that while he is programming, he and the assistant will be processing orders (welding and grinding bumpers), so the company will be making money off these machines while the programming continues."

Poor Jonathan was doing all the talking and none of the eating. The waitress came over to our table and asked if there was anything else that she could get us. I told her no. I finished my breakfast and did not want another cup of coffee. I told Jonathan to take his time and finish his omelet. Fifteen minutes later, the waitress brought me the check for the breakfast. I added the tip, signed it, and put my room number on the invoice. We all got up, and 15 minutes later, Suzanne parked the Bronco by the front door of the facilities.

When I walked in the front door to the showroom, I could not believe my eyes. The room looked nothing like what it looked like two weeks ago. Jonathan and Suzanne described what they had done to the room, but their words did not accurately depict what I was looking at. The place looked beautiful! It was impressive! The five cars in the showroom were all done, detailed, and looked like new offroad vehicles. All five were in a straight row on the right side of the room. The other three older cars were not there anymore. Then, the older cars Jonathan had stored somewhere did not look more aged. They all looked like they were still new. Large, very professional posters on the walls advertised all the different vendors' offroad products that their company sells.

The floor shined. It looked brand new. I knew I had to make a fuss over the whole room because my two clients worked their tails off, making the showroom this beautiful. I sat my backpack down on one of the tables in the room and pulled out a tablet to make some notes. The first note was to take professional-grade pictures of this room from all angles and post them on their website. Then, eventually, post them on Facebook plus other social media sites. I wanted the public, vendors, and customers to see what this company's showroom looks like now. As beautiful as it is, I was sure the upgrading effort would generate new customer orders. I felt like I had to control my emotions about the changes in the room, or I would look silly in front of the two owners.

I followed Suzanne into her office because I wanted to set my backpack on the table where I would work for the day. Then, I would take a tour of the rest of the building. When I got to the office, it looked as beautiful as the showroom. All the junk in the office two weeks ago was gone. Like the showroom, they waxed her office floor to shine like a mirror. Her desk was neat and organized. There were also vendor advertisements on the walls. I was so impressed. I put my backpack on the conference room table and asked Jonathan to show me all the other changes since I was here last. He nodded yes, and I followed him out of her office. He went into the showroom and straight to the door leading into the shop. He walked over to where the four robots were to introduce me to the new programmer. I was following Jonathan when George, the cutter operator, saw me. He quickly shook my hand and said, "Hello." He said, "Bob, I hope you have five free minutes to chat with me today."

I told George I would find time to visit him sometime today. I enjoyed George. He was one of the good guys. Then, when we got to the welder's area, the new programmer was unloading a bumper off the fully programmed robotic welder. He put the bumper on a dolly and removed his gloves so we could shake hands. Jonathan said, "Herman, I want to introduce you to Bob Curry. He is the guy I told you about helping us improve the production output in the shop." Once again, my title changed for this client to the "Production Output" guy! Herman said, "Bob, it is nice to meet you, sir. I have heard nothing but good things about your work here!" I responded, "Herman, I am so happy you are here. We needed these machines to weld and grind our bumpers, not sit here and collect dust." "Bob, I assure you that all these robotic machines will kick butt in the next seven to ten days. These machines are top-of-the-line for robotic welders and grinders. As I get a bumper model programmed, we then process all the customer orders for that model bumper on the customer order backlog report." I asked Herman, "How many more bumpers do we have customer orders for still needing to be programmed?" He said, "I honestly don't have that number for you. I will pull the report, sort it by bumper model, and let you know. I can tell you; it is my experience over the years, that these machines are lightning fast, and the quality of the welds is excellent." "If that is the case, Herman, why is the company that Jonathan purchased the equipment from not able to have their programmer here to do the work you are doing?" "Bob, I understand they have so many orders for the machines that they cannot keep up with them. I have heard that their sales are up by 200% over last year's numbers." I told

Herman, "That is a good and terrible thing, all simultaneously. It sounds like they are selling great machines to their customers, but the company cannot service these great welders due to labor problems for the programming." "That is probably a very accurate description of that company's problems," said Herman. "Mr. Curry, they probably need someone like you to go there and clean up their operations and service departments!" I responded, "Herman, please call me Bob. Mr. Curry was my father, and he passed away in 1980.

When Herman and I finished our conversation, Jonathan took me on a tour of the rest of the shop. Jonathan explained that he and all the employees working in the shop got together and discussed a new layout for the whole shop area. They planned to have each fabrication station's staging area next to the machine. They planned to paint a thick yellow box around the perimeter to organize the space. After completing the fabrication for the bumper at that station, they would move it to the next station, right next to the last station. There were seven stations, and they planned to put a landing area to stage the bumpers with enough room for the equipment and its operator. The shop guys worked on one station every evening for three hours after 5:00 p.m. So far, they had one station done, and it looked great. They even painted the yellow box around the perimeter." Jonathan next took me over to the warehousing and shipping area. When we got there, Jake and I shook hands. Jonathan asked Jake to explain all the changes they had made to his shipping area. Jake pulled a drawing from his desk drawer and showed me the schematic. I could see that Jake was proud and excited about the new layout of his area. They scheduled Jake's area as the last station for the shop team to get together after work and reorganize his shipping area. Jake said he would be more efficient shipping bumpers after reorganizing his space.

Jonathan also told me he had called the manufacturers of all the equipment in the shop to make preventive maintenance service calls in the next 30 days. Jonathan said, "Bob if one of our machines goes down, it stops all our shipping to our customers. If it doesn't stop it, it severely slows it down. In the recent meeting with the shop guys, we set a goal with the group to get the backlog of customer orders down to three weeks or lower by year-end. If that happens, I told the group they could all plan to receive their first-ever Christmas bonus this year. That statement put some big smiles on everyone's face in that meeting." Jonathan said that our tour of the shop was over. I was glad because the shop had no air conditioning, and I started sweating in the heat. I wanted to return to the air-conditioned office area as soon as possible.

I first walked over to the cutter machine to find George. I shook his hand again and asked what he wanted to talk about. He said, "Bob, I must give you a big pat on the back. Since you left here a couple of weeks ago, the employees have been buzzing around in the shop like never before. The company's morale amongst the employees has never been higher. When you were here before, this shop's production was terrible. Based on my machine's production, I have cut out parts for twice the bumpers I did during any week in the past year. The welding group has kept up with my machine's production. I am shocked. Also, the boys here are getting along well with the new computer programmer. He is genuinely nice and knows what he is doing with those robots. I asked George, "What do you think about the plans to reorganize the layout of the shop?" George said, "Bob, that move is overdue. We should have reorganized this place back when

Jonathan bought those four robots. The vendor delivered the four machines, and Jonathan stuck them in an empty spot in the shop. What a dumb thing to do when fabricating big heavy metal bumpers. The less you have to move those bumpers around, the better." "So, George, what I hear you saying is things are going well here in the last two weeks." He nodded yes. I shook his hand again and headed to the showroom after I thanked him for his time.

When I returned to the showroom, Jonathan said he had one more area to show me. We walked over to the men's bathroom, and he opened the door for me to see inside. Unlike many other men's rooms, I have been in recently, the bathroom looked great. It smelled pleasant. They did the floors and painted the walls and the stalls. The sinks and mirrors looked so clean that they appeared brand new. The bathrooms on my first trip here were so bad that I decided not to use them. I waited until I got back to my hotel room to relieve myself.

*   *   *

Jonathan and I returned to Suzanne's office, and I sat at the table and got my computer out to start working. I planned to review all the PIR action plans. I wanted to check the finished tasks and which ones still need work. I wanted to ensure that Jonathan and Suzanne did not drop the ball on any essential functions with the list of the 15 PIRs in their notebooks.

PIR #1 – Dress for Success – 100% Completed. It was an instant success with the owners. Suzanne picked out the uniforms and did a fantastic job with her choices.

PIR #2 – Let the buyer make the first offer if you are selling your company – Not started – It was not necessary to begin until the company was ready to be up for sale again.

PIR #3 – Keep the shop, showroom, offices, parking lot, vehicles, and bathrooms clean and looking professional. – 66% Completed – They still need to finish doing the new layout in the shop. They should complete it all in less than two weeks from today. The shop's new layout will increase productivity.

PIR #4 – Thinking out-of-the-box to improve the cash flow – 50% completed – Jonathan has an excellent start on meeting the general managers at the local car dealerships to sell them Utah Off-road bumpers. The goal is to show our products in the dealership showrooms. He met with the Jeep and Lexus general managers and has Ford and Toyota appointments scheduled for this week.

PIR #5 – Seek tax advice from your tax expert. – Not started yet.

PIR #6 – Seventeen-year-old son and video games do not belong in a fabrication shop. – 100% completed, thank goodness!

PIR #7 – Four robotic machines are not operating in the shop. – 50% completed – Jonathan has found and hired a very experienced and skilled programmer from Weber State. Jonathan also contacted the equipment manufacturer, invoiced them as per the programming reimbursement agreement, and received $14,400 to pay for the programming costs.

PIR #8 – Meet with the owner of the powder coating vendor to improve the quality and production of their services – 75% completed – Jonathan and Jake met with the company's owner and got four weeks of powder coating production for free to make up for the lost costs of the company's poor prior output. The company's owner committed to staying in Utah to resolve the powder coating production problem.

PIR #9 – Research the local market salary for welders – Not started yet.

PIR #10 – Recruit one of the adjunct instructors from WSU with computer programming knowledge – 100% completed.

PIR #11 – Meet with the head of the manufacturing engineering technology program at WSU and offer the university a welding intern program at their shop – Not started yet.

PIR #12 – Hire a strong supervisor to manage all the shop employees directly – Not started yet.

PIR #13 – Hire two laborers to work in the shop to move products – Not started yet.

PIR #14 – Create a production incentive plan to incentivize and motivate the shop staff – 25% completed – Jonathan offered the shop staff a bonus if they got the customer order backlog report down to three weeks of production or less by year-end. The incentive plan needs decisions about the bonus amount and when to pay the employees.

PIR #15 – Create installation instructions for every product sold to customers and included with each shipment. – 25% completed.

I was delighted and surprised with the company's accomplishments over the past ten days. Jonathan and Suzanne have kicked butt, much to my surprise. While I am here during this visit, I need to ensure this level of progress continues. The list of 15 PIRs was perfect to get them motivated. They focused on the right PIRs, thank goodness. My priority was to increase the shop's production, lowering the backlog of customer orders from six months to three or fewer weeks. The substantial progress in programming the robots and increasing production is the most considerable success.

I must be at this location every other week to ensure they stay focused. During this trip, I plan to work on and review their financial statements. By working in the economic area of the company, I would not be taking up any of Jonathan's or Suzanne's time or attention.

While sitting at the table, I wondered why so much progress had occurred during the past ten days. Two weeks ago, the place looked like a total dump. It dawned on me that neither of the two owners are leaders. They both have a "follower" type of personality. They are both looking for a leader to follow and make their business successful. The operation of those four robotic machines is the most significant impact on this business's success. Those four machines sat there for over six months collecting dust rather than Jonathan taking charge and fixing the problem. Fixing that problem this past week took minimal time and effort. The powder coating company could have been a better vendor with better service and a faster turnaround time for each bumper. Jonathan wrote off the problem by saying, "They are not that bad, and I have other bigger problems to deal with right now." And then, to fix the problem, it only took a phone call to the owner of the company and an hour-long meeting. The result of the meeting was a commitment from the owner that he would fix the problem immediately, plus Jonathan's company would get the next month's powder coating service for free. Now that I have recognized no leadership talents with either of the two owners, I need to deal with and resolve this problem as the business turnaround specialist.

If this company had a strong leader managing the business, it would have looked materially different two weeks ago at my first meeting with the owners. Some of the differences would have been:

1. The showroom, offices, shop, and bathrooms would always look like they do now compared to the mess they were in when I first arrived on my initial visit.

2. The showroom would never have had the five vehicles with the original bumpers removed lying on the floor. Working on the cars one at a time and keeping the showroom beautiful was the simple answer to the problem.

3. The physical layout of the shop would have been more efficient if the staff had rearranged the fabrication stations' machinery months ago.

4. The backlog of customer orders would be two or three weeks rather than six months.

5. The robots could have been working six months ago rather than sitting there like four dust collectors all this time.

6. The powder coating vendor would have an excellent history of powder coating without any problems and turning around the bumpers in two or three days.

7. The shipment of every bumper would include installation instructions.

8. Properly staff the shop with the right number of employees with little or no employee turnover. The company should pay the welders at the current market salary for certified welders.

9. The annual sales would be two or three times what they are today, and the company would be very profitable.

I spent the rest of the day developing a plan for dealing with the leadership problem for the client. In my current PIRs, two action plans are to hire a shop supervisor and controller. I will take charge of selecting the candidates for both positions for this company in the next two months. If we can find suitable candidates for those two positions, we could have a strong leader in the shop and one in the office and financial areas of the company. If I can hire the right people for these two management positions, the right managers will resolve the company's leadership problems. I wrote a PIR for this leadership problem but did not plan to distribute it to the owners.

Chapter 8

THE NUMBERS!

"If you don't have regular and accurate financial statements, you're driving your business 100 miles per hour down a one-way street the wrong way, at night, in the fog, without lights."
— JIM BLASINGAME – AN AMERICAN SMALL BUSINESS EXPERT, RADIO TALK SHOW HOST, AUTHOR, AND SYNDICATED COLUMNIST

Tuesday, August 23rd – Day 5 of week 2
of the turnaround engagement

THE TWO OWNERS ARRIVED AT THE RESTAURANT right on time at 7:55 a.m. for our regularly scheduled breakfast. I asked them if they had anything new to report about successes with the 15 PIRs. Suzanne said she had received several resumes for the shop supervisor and the controller positions. She also said she had received five resumes for the two laborer positions I had recommended for the shop. Jonathan said, "Bob, I am concerned about our cash position if we hire all these positions immediately. Your plan to accomplish all the PIRs will generate lots of cash. But, until we do, hiring people raises my stress level, and you know what happens when my stress is up. When my blood pressure rises, I get grumpy. I need to see a big cluster of customer orders to stabilize my blood pressure and irritability." I responded, "Jonathan, we will not make our future business decisions based on your blood pressure or grumpy level. We will make good, sound business decisions based on facts, accurate data, monthly financial statements, and budgets."

Suzanne, please email me the most current financial statements. I will need the following:

1. Last two years of income statements by month,

2. The year-end balance sheet for each year,

3. The current year's income statements by month and the balance sheets,

4. This year's and next year's annual budget.

5. Any operating reports generated for the shop operations.

6. Your last two years' income tax returns for Utah Off-road.

7. And accounts payable and accounts receivable aging reports."

Suzanne had her small tablet out and was making a list of all my requests. She said she could have all that information to me as soon as we arrived at the office. She added, "Bob, we don't have any budgets, but we do have a business plan from two years ago developed for the business. I think you will like it and it will be beneficial. And if Karla comes in today, I will ask her to sit with you to explain all the numbers for you." "That would be great, but what does Karla do for the company?" "She is our bookkeeper. She also prepares all the bills for payment and cuts the checks. She collects the receivables when they come due. I need to call her and find out if she is coming to the office today. Recently, she had both knees replaced, and she does not get along that well anymore. Karla is overweight, which puts huge pressure on her knees. She sits at her desk all day when she comes to the office. She eats her lunch at her desk, so she does not put any pressure on her new knees during the day." "Suzanne," I asked, "Do all your customers prepay for their bumper orders?" "Yes, Bob, that is right, but we extend credit to some of the dealers we sell to. We give them 30-day terms to allow them to collect the payment for the orders from their customers before we get paid. But because we have a 26-week order backlog, we get very few orders from dealers. I am talking about dealers like your friends, Brian and Jordon, at ABC Off-road Supply."

Suzanne immediately called Karla and found out she was not coming to work today because she did not feel well. She did not want to go to work today because she had lost her cane at her home and could not find it yet.

I looked at Jonathan and said, "Jonathan, I expect to materially grow this business by selling to the dealers all over the United States once we get our production up and our customer order backlog down. We need to develop a marketing brochure for the business that we can mail or email to every offroad distributor in the United States before the end of the fourth quarter. But, and I mean but, we need to have confidence in our ability to produce the bumpers much quicker. If our sales triple in the first quarter of next year, I don't want this shop to slip back to a huge backlog of customer orders." Suzanne commented, "We have a beautiful brochure we designed about a year ago but never mailed it out." I said, "I am sure the brochure is genuinely nice, but it does not have the message I want it to deliver to our distributor customers. Because of the company's terrible reputation for how extremely slowly we deliver customer orders, I want a large banner on the front of the new brochure. Our company now ships our customers' orders within two weeks after the company receives and confirms the orders. I want to put the mirror image message on our website: "We ship all customer orders within two weeks after we receive them, and the order is confirmed." Jonathan said, "And Bob, what happens if we cannot reach that goal?" I answered him while looking him straight in the eyes, "Jonathan, I have been doing this type of consulting for over 20 years. I have tackled problems for businesses much larger than this company. Producing these bumpers is not a challenging task."

"I got on my computer last night and researched all the different offroad bumper manufacturers in the US. Only about half of manufacturers had on their website how long the customers would have to wait for their orders. The other 50% said nothing about a delivery date. I called half of those companies and asked them if I placed my order today for a bumper, when can I expect to receive the shipment? Most companies said by September 15th, which included the delivery time. Three companies said they would ship the bumper before September 1st if I gave them the order today. September 1st is seven days from today! So, what my research revealed last night was that the industry for offroad bumpers is manufacturing and shipping customer orders in one to three weeks. All the companies said they would ship the order in up to three weeks. So, the question popped into my head: What are we doing wrong? I went back and reviewed my notes from the PIRs. I am 100% convinced that this company can upgrade the shop's policies, procedures, and production to at least match our competitors' order shipment schedule."

"Jonathan, since my first day here, I never once thought what would happen if I failed. I have never thought about failing. Failing is not an option with my clients. If you follow my direction and the PIRs, I will commit that we will not fail. Because of the immense upside of your offroad products, the opportunity to increase sales is what I would call a sales explosion! This company is selling next to nothing to all the offroad distributors in the USA. When we grow to be successful with selling to the distributors in the US, we can start selling to Canada, Australia, and all through Europe." Jonathan sat there quietly for at least a minute, a long minute. Finally, he said, "You are a big thinker! I hoped we could start shipping faster to slow down the customer complaints. You are talking about shipping all over the world. What a substantial difference!" "Jonathan, I don't have any history of failing, so I am not particularly good at it. Business owners hire me because I can quickly identify what is wrong with the business. Then, I developed a plan to fix the problems immediately. If you are nervous about us not being successful, call Brian and Jordan. Ask them if we had any failures during my consulting engagement with ABC Off-road Supply." "Bob, I know you were very successful, per all my conversations with Brian over the past year." "Good, then let's remove the word "failure" from our conversations starting today!"

"The other way that we will grow the sales is to inform all the potential offroad customers on our website and social media that when they order anything from this company, they will receive the product within 21 days or less. Our goal is to ship all customer orders within 14 days. As soon as we finish all the action items with the 15 PIRs, I am sure we will be shipping all products within two weeks, and never more."

I told Jonathan and Suzanne, "Let's get to the office. I have a lot of work to do to analyze the company's financial statements and develop a budget for the rest of this year and the next 12 months. We need to have accurate financial statements while we are going through this transition with the company. We need to know where we are financially and our exact cash position. Do the two of you trust the monthly financial records that Karla gives you?" Jonathan said, "Bob, are you kidding? Our financial statements are a joke. Karla is a minimum-wage bookkeeper who couldn't be much better at her job. She is so bad that she does not even know how bad she is. And that is when she shows up at the office to do her job. When we gave our income statement and year-end balance sheet to our tax guy, he was distraught with us. He said the income statement was off by hundreds of thousands of dollars. He threatened that he would not do our tax return in the future unless we fixed our "Karla" problem soon. He said that unless we find someone who had a clue about what Generally Accepted Accounting Principles ("GAAP") are, he was not going to put his firm at risk with the IRS." I sat there listening and could not believe what I was hearing from the owner of my client. I asked Jonathan when your tax guy gave you the unpleasant facts about Karla. Suzanne answered, "Bob, that was the week before you arrived for your first visit. I could not believe a CPA could get so emotional about a client's tax return." "Suzanne, your company's tax returns put your tax preparer's firm at risk. The IRS could fine his firm and not accept any more tax returns with his signature on the bottom of a tax return as the tax preparer. I can understand him being upset at the two of you! Let's get to the office now; I have more work to do than I first planned."

While we were riding there, I could not believe that a $3,200,000 company would hire a "bargain-basement, minimum wage" bookkeeper to keep their books. The two owners of this company have made some terrible decisions in managing this business, but this one was the worst.

*   *   *

When we arrived, I went straight to Suzanne's office. I asked her to email me all the financial statements, tax returns, and operational reports I requested at breakfast as soon as possible. Suzanne emailed me everything I asked for, plus she printed hard copies of all the information and filed them in a binder with dividers for me. She also emailed me the business plan written two years ago.

After hearing how upset the company's tax preparer was at Jonathan and Suzanne, I decided I needed to do something quickly. His complaint was due to the lack of accuracy in the company's financial statements. I planned to immediately clean up this year's income statement and balance sheet.

I knew in South Florida, there is an organization called "B2BCFO". It stands for "Business to Business Chief Financial Officer." This organization has mostly retired CFOs or controllers who no longer want to work full-time. They usually take on a client or two and work at their office one or two days a week to keep the financial records current and accurate. A company like Utah Off-road is the perfect type of client for B2BCFO, and B2BCFO is the ideal organization for my client. A person from the organization could come to the office and initially work two to five days a week to clean up the financial records.

I talked to Jonathan and Suzanne about my idea of replacing Karla initially with someone from the B2BCFO organization and then hiring a full-time controller, if necessary. They loved the idea. I called the local B2BCFO office and asked if I could have someone in the area come to our office to interview for the job this afternoon. The person who answered the call (Sue) asked me how many candidates I wanted to interview this afternoon. I said I wanted to talk to two or three people for the job. Sue said she could have one person at our offices at 12:30, one at 3:00, and the last at 4:00 p.m. She told me that all their candidates have had successful background checks and been drug tested. She said that she would email me each of their resumes.

When I hung up on the *B2BCFO* phone call, I felt like I had just hit a home run for this client to fix a significant problem with the company. I received copies of the resumes of the three candidates and reviewed each. Two of them had worked for many years for a manufacturer, and the third had well-rounded experience with several different companies, including a CPA firm. All three of them were excellent candidates. I decided to interview the three people initially. I would then ask Suzanne to meet and ask the best candidate any questions that she may have. I also chose not to tell Jonathan to participate in the interview process. He would not know what to ask the person because he knows nothing about accounting or financial statements.

At 12:20, the first candidate showed up at the front door and told one of the employees from the customer service department that she was looking for Bob Curry. The customer service department is located right inside the front door of the showroom. Olivia, one of the two customer service employees, walked the lady to Suzanne's office, where I worked at the conference table.

I introduced myself while we were shaking hands. I explained that I was here as a business consultant to upgrade all areas of the company. I told her that my role was to increase shop production, grow the company's sales, and improve the timeliness and accuracy of the financial statements.

The candidate's name was Jennifer. Jennifer was in her early to mid-fifties and looked in great shape for her age. She wore a black business suit with a light blue blouse under the suit coat. Jennifer seemed very professional and would be a fantastic addition to the office staff. We sat at the table, and she told me about her career without me asking. Jennifer was happy to be in this interview. She said her home is less than one mile from the office. She also seemed like a happy person in general, which was a good thing.

She commented on how beautiful the showroom and Suzanne's office were. My response to her was that if she had been here two weeks ago, she would have never made that statement. She looked at me with a very confused look. I understood her confusion. Anyone who saw the beautiful showroom's status and Suzanne's office would not have believed how bad the two rooms were just two weeks ago.

Jennifer shared with me that she had just started with *B2BCFO,* and this was her first interview. The company, her prior employer, relocated, and their offices moved from Salt Lake City to another state. She said she took a year off because she received an excellent severance package. She added that she worked 50 to 60 hours a week at the company and took some time off to recover from working so hard for so long. Jennifer worked for that organization for over 20 years.

She started there as an accountant and became the CFO five years before the owners decided to sell the company.

She said that she was confident that she would be able to handle the job well, as I described it. I decided then that I would introduce her to Suzanne. Suzanne came into her office and introduced herself to Jennifer. The two talked for 30 minutes and got along like they had known each other for several years.

During the interview, I asked Jennifer several accounting questions. She immediately convinced me that she knew accounting, financial statements, payroll procedures, GAAP, corporate tax filings, etc. During the interview, I rated her accounting knowledge a ten out of a possible ten. Suzanne told me that she hoped I would hire Jennifer because she thought that Jennifer was excellent. I called the *B2BCFO* office immediately and asked Sue to cancel the other two interviews because we wanted to offer Jennifer the job. Sue said that Jennifer would be incredibly happy to hear our decision. Sue noted that Jennifer just called her and said she loved the company. I told her we would like her to come to the office tomorrow, Thursday, and Friday. I want her to work here every day next week because we have a lot of work to catch up on. Sue said she would call Jennifer right back and tell her to report to our office at 9:00 a.m. tomorrow. I told Sue I would be at the office most of the day tomorrow. My flight home is at 7:00 p.m. on Wednesday.

Suzanne was happy with the whole transaction with Jennifer. She was also pleased she could eliminate Karla, which she had wanted to do for months. I suggested to Suzanne that she call Karla and tell her I found her replacement since she has not felt well since the knee replacement. Suzanne called her immediately. After the call, Suzanne told me that

Karla was so pleased we found her replacement. Karla said she wanted to quit for months but did not want to hurt the company. Suzanne said, "Hmm…if she only knew the truth!"

After Suzanne's comment, I thought she should have known the truth because Suzanne is one of the company's two owners. I told Suzanne, "You should not have accepted Karla's sub-standard work." After pondering the whole situation, I decided to talk to Suzanne about the entire problem with Karla. I said, "Suzanne, I believe you should have talked to Karla about her poor performance handling the company's financial department. It would have been best if you had given her a performance review to let her know she was not doing her job well. It would help if you had given her a deadline to improve; if she didn't, you would replace her. She felt comfortable taking days off even though there was a huge backlog of work in the financial department at your company. The company cannot afford to have inaccurate financial statements. Financial statements are an essential part of this business. Karla was not the right person for the job. Both you and Jonathan knew that and did nothing about it. Even after your tax preparer threatened that he would not do your tax returns, you still did nothing about the problem. You cannot afford to have weak employees with a company this size. Having your weakest employee in charge of your financial records is bad!"

"Bob, you are right. I should have dealt with the problem a long time ago rather than sticking my head in the sand, hoping that the problem would go away someday." "Well, Suzanne, your problems don't just go away. You and Jonathan need to step up and deal with each problem. That is why I wrote the 15 PIRs. Writing them up as I did, rating the problems on a one to ten scale, prioritizing each, and assigning a deadline is a good example of dealing with the company's problems. Now, you and Jonathan must pull your heads out of the sand and deal with each other."

When I was alone in the office working on the financial statements, I could not believe how poor an employee Karla was. It is hard to believe the two owners just accepted her abysmal performance. Then, I figured out the real problem. Jonathan and Suzanne were both nervous about adding people to the organization's payroll and the level of salary they pay for each position. They try to find the cheapest candidate to hire regardless of their skills. The owners were paying her the minimum legal wage in Utah, so her inferior performance in doing her job was acceptable. It is okay because they got her to work for such a low wage at the company. Their business philosophy about hiring employees and my philosophy on hiring people are 180° different. I believe:

"The way to make money in business is to hire the best people in the area, treat them with respect, give them the tools to do their job, provide them an excellent environment to work in, and compensate them fairly."

Next, I had to put together a "Task List" for Jennifer when she arrives to start her new job tomorrow morning.

The task list needed to be more formal. After I went home, I compiled the list to discuss all I wanted Jennifer to accomplish. I will not return to this office for 11 days, Monday, September 5th. I knew that Jonathan and Suzanne would be unable to give her any help or direction while I was gone. I scheduled a Zoom call for this Friday, next Tuesday, and Thursday while I was home. I don't want her to get stuck and start spinning her wheels while I am in Florida. After my interview with her, I am confident in her accounting skills.

Utah Off-road Manufacturing
Accounting/Financial Statements Task List
Date: August 23, 20XX

Project - Prior two years and Current year Income Statements, Balance Sheets, and Budget.	
#	Task Description
1	Reformate the financial statements.
2	Create a general ledger analysis for each BS account & reconcile it to each of your month-end closings.
3	Verify the YE balance sheet from last year used by the tax preparer to the openning balances for this year.
4	Create an Income Statement and Balance Sheet for each month from January to August.
5	Create a one-page monthly analysis for each month recapping the highlight issues for each month.
6	Create a monthly graph showing monthly sales, Gross Profit, Gross Profit %, Payroll, and Pre-Tax Profit.
7	Create a binder divided into 12 monthly sections each for the monthly reports after each has been completed.
8	Create a month end closing package for the owners to review and understand.
9	Reformate the two prior year's Income Statements and Balance Sheets.
10	Create a three year Income Statement and Balance Sheet comparison of the three years.
11	Create a budget for the current year and next year by month.

For the rest of the day, I reviewed everything accomplished with all the action plans for all 15 PIRs. I made another task list for the action items I wanted Jonathan and Suzanne to complete, much like the one I made for Jennifer. I needed the two owners to accomplish as much with this list between my visits as they accomplished between this and my first visit. The one critical issue that I want them to focus on is hiring a supervisor for the shop.

Late in the day, Suzanne came to see me about scheduling interviews for the three candidates for the shop supervisor position. She gave me a copy of each of their resumes to review. She asked if I wanted her to schedule an interview with each of them tomorrow. I told her I would enjoy meeting the three candidates because I look forward to having a supervisor in the shop. As we discussed, we need a strong manager who knows what he is doing in a manufacturing environment. I asked her if she could schedule the interviews tomorrow at 12:00 noon, 1:00 p.m., and 2:00 p.m. I told Suzanne I planned to spend the morning with Jennifer from *B2BCPO*. I want to give her a good "onboarding" to this company plus get her started working with the financial statements. I told Suzanne I would need her to ensure she had a clean desk with a phone and a computer. She will need an email address and password for all her programs. Suzanne said she would clean Karla's desk and put together a list of all the passwords, etc. I continued, "Jennifer will need a firm understanding of what I would like her to do until I return to Utah on Monday, a week and a half from now.

I told Suzanne I suggested not scheduling an interview for the candidates applying for the controller position. I want to see how well Jennifer does in the financial department. If she is highly qualified and successful at cleaning up the financial statements for this company, she might want a permanent position. It is excellent that Jennifer lives less than a mile from the office. Hiring Jennifer could work out very well because after she cleans up the accounting records, she will have an intimate knowledge of this company and everything in the finance department.

Suzanne asked me if I was still interested in hiring a laborer or two for the shop. I told her I was okay with hiring one laborer and holding off on the second one. I want to see if we can reorganize the shop and keep overtime to a minimum. Not only that, if we hire someone who will be a "keeper," that employee could run the bender that your son was babysitting.

Suzanne said that she would talk to Jonathan about the issue. He would be in favor of hiring one laborer/machine operator. It is a promising idea for that person to be responsible for running the bender. When he does not have to be there to operate the bender, he can help around in the shop, moving the finished bumpers to the next fabrication staging areas. Suzanne asked if I would be interested in interviewing the candidates for the laborer position. I told Suzanne my day is full tomorrow, working with Jennifer and interviewing the shop supervisor candidates. Then Suzanne hustled off to schedule the appointments and whatever else she was working on.

At 4:30 p.m., Suzanne came to her office and asked if I needed a ride back to the hotel. I had two options: walk or ride with Suzanne. I took the second option! I saved everything that I was working on with my computer. I put my laptop and the binder Suzanne made for me earlier today in my backpack. When I returned to my room, I reviewed the financial statements and noted where I thought the problems were. Later that evening, I went downstairs, got dinner, and turned in early. I was tired.

Chapter 9

HIRE THE BEST!

"The key for us, number one, has always been hiring very smart people."
— BILL GATES – AN AMERICAN BUSINESS MAGNATE, INVESTOR, PHILANTHROPIST, AND CO-FOUNDER OF SOFTWARE GIANT MICROSOFT.

Wednesday, August 24th – Day 6 of week 2 of the turnaround engagement

I WAS UP VERY EARLY THIS MORNING BECAUSE I have a lot of work to accomplish before I fly home this evening. I plan to organize myself this morning for a very efficient day. I need to spend the morning with Jennifer from *B2BCFO* to get her onboard with the company and help her start cleaning up the financial statements. I created a task list for the project for her to follow. *(See page #191.)* Our interview yesterday gave me great confidence that she could easily handle the responsibilities of this company's controller position and this cleanup project. The ideal situation would have been for her to start earlier in the week (Monday) when I arrived in Utah. I could have had more time with her at the start of the project. But, just like the old *Rolling Stones* song, *"You can't always get what you want!"* I will train Jennifer for half a day today to show her how I want everything done. Then, she will be alone except for our future Zoom calls between my visits. That way, I can answer any of her questions."

Starting at noon, 1 p.m., and 2 p.m. today, I am interviewing the three candidates for the shop supervisor position. The combination of these positions, controller and shop supervisor, is critical to this client's turnaround. Because, as I stated before, neither of the owners are leaders. Therefore, I need to hire leaders to handle the front end of the business, including the financial department and the shop.

At 7:50 a.m., I waited for Jonathan and Suzanne in the restaurant with my usual cup of hot coffee. Ten minutes later, the two owners entered the restaurant and sat at my table. There is something different about these two people since my first visit to Utah and this visit. I do not know what caused the change, but I hope they never revert to their old ways.

Jonathan said, "Good morning, Bob. How are you doing this fine morning?" "Jonathan, I am doing great; thank you for asking!" Suzanne asked me, "How did you do with Jennifer yesterday? Did you get her commitment to come to our company and work with us to clean up Karla's work?" "Suzanne, I did. She is excited to work with you. The two of you looked like you got along very well together. I gave her a verbal test concerning her accounting skills, and she passed excellently. I hope she does an excellent job cleaning the financial records and is interested in a permanent position with your company. Did I tell you she lives less than one mile from your facilities? Her resume for the controller position is excellent. Jonathan asked, "So, Bob, I assume she is on a "rent to buy program" with her company. In other words, we can hire her part-time to upgrade our financial statements.

After she has completed that project, we can either:

1. Keep her part-time.

2. Hire her full-time.

3. Thank her for her excellent work and end the relationship.

"Jonathan, that is exactly right. This situation with Jennifer is a perfect way to hire a senior manager for your organization. You get to see and experience her work to determine if she is another "Karla" or a superstar to add to your staff. She will fit in very well with your current employees and Suzanne. She will be able to handle all the duties in her position as the controller for your company." Suzanne spoke up and said, "Bob, I could not agree more. I love the fact that she lives so close to our offices."

I continued, "She is going to be a key hire for the company, but the position I want to fill as soon as possible is the shop supervisor. We need someone with experience working in a welding shop who is a certified welder. We need that person to be a strong leader and control all the employees manufacturing offroad bumpers in your shop. We need this person also to have computer programming skills. It is a shame that no firms like *B2BCFO* exist, only for welding shop supervisors."

"Bob, in case we don't have time to meet today since you have such a busy day, what do you want Suzanne and me to work on until you return for your next visit?" "Jonathan, excellent question! It is straightforward, though. You both have a list of the PIRs and all the action plan steps. All the PIRs are essential. The ones with the highest rating are the most important. I aim to increase production and manufacture more bumpers with the same or better quality but two or three times faster. As I see it, the following are the ones that the two of you and the guys in the shop should focus on while I am away.

1. Create installation instructions for every product sold. – These installation instructions are vital so we can stop the calls to the customer service department from all the unhappy customers not knowing how to install their bumpers. This PIR should be Jonathan's #1 priority.

2. Hire the right person to be the shop supervisor with a start date as soon as possible.

3. Finish programming the robotic welders and grinders for every bumper we sell.

4. Finish rearranging the shop layout to be the most efficient possible.

5. Keep your eye on the powder coating company to ensure the quality of their services is as good as the company owner promised.

6. Finish visiting all the car dealerships' general managers in the area to sell offroad products for their vehicles and display them in their showrooms.

7. Start selling the vehicles in the showroom to generate cash for the business.

When I am not here, you may call me any time. I am here to serve the two of you during this consulting engagement. I am here to grow this company's sales, improve production, upgrade the management, reduce employee turnover, and get the financial statements under control, current and accurate. Then, of course, improve cash flow by increasing the profits. So, let's get a quick breakfast and get to the office. I have an appointment with Jennifer at 9:00 a.m.

*　　*　　*

We arrived at 8:45 a.m., 15 minutes before I expected Jennifer to arrive at the front door for her first day at Utah Off-road. I walked into Suzanne's office and unpacked my computer from my backpack. As I plugged my laptop into the wall outlet, I looked up. Jennifer had entered the office and was standing right next to me. I was slightly surprised because I did not hear her walk into the office, plus she was ten minutes early.

Jennifer said, "Good morning, Mr. Curry. Is this where we are going to work today?" "Yes, because Suzanne needs more time to clean up the bookkeeper's desk, where you will be sitting after today." Jennifer pulled her laptop computer out of her briefcase and set it up on the opposite side of the table from where mine was sitting. She also pulled out a notebook and a pen. She then took off her suit jacket, put it on the back of her chair, and sat down. I did the same.

Jennifer said, "I am sorry for calling you Mr. Curry. I did that at my interview yesterday, and you asked me to call you Bob. I promise you that I will not make that mistake again in the future." I responded, "No big deal, Jennifer!" She then opened her notebook with at least a full page of handwritten notes. She said, "Rather than tell me how you want the financial statements cleaned up, I wrote my outline of how I would pursue the project and then see if you agree with my procedure." I smiled at her because I liked that she took charge of the project rather than waiting for me to "spoon-feed" her on what and how to do it. I sat back in my chair and said, "Great!"

She started, "First, I will ask for the year-end worksheets from the tax preparer and begin with the balance sheet accounts he used for the tax return. I will create a trial balance for each of the balance sheet accounts. Bob, I learned from my Accounting 101 professor in college a long time ago, "During the month-end closing, if you prove the balance sheet is right, the income statement has to be right." So, during the closings, I always go down the assets, followed by the liabilities, and accurately reconcile them. Once my general ledger analysis is accurate every month, the closings are effortless and quick.

Then, starting with cash, I will create a "general ledger analysis" for each account. I will get the December and January bank statements from Suzanne and ensure the reconciliations are accurate. I will verify that the bookkeeper made all the adjusting journal entries from the reconciliation and posted them to the cash account. I will file the bank reconciliations in my general ledger analysis binder. Next, I will get a copy of the accounts receivable from Suzanne and verify all those balances. If there are any delinquent accounts, I will call that customer to collect any receivables over 60 days old. I will add an aged accounts receivable trial balance to my general analysis binder, along with notes about the delinquent accounts. Then, I will go through the same process for any prepaid assets. I will pull out the insurance policies to review the coverages and the premiums. If I find any problems with the insurance policies, I will deal with them immediately. Then, I will add a copy of the insurance policy and my prepaid asset calculations to my binder. If I am lucky, the tax preparer will have all the fixed asset schedules with the depreciation/amortization calculations.

I said, "Jennifer, let me interrupt you here. From what I understand, this company's bookkeeper treated all payments for customer orders as a sale rather than a deposit against a future sale. Since this company has a six-month customer order backlog, those payments should be in the customer deposit account, a liability, on the balance sheet. Only when the product is manufactured and shipped to the customer can the sale be recorded." Jennifer said, "So you are saying the company has overstated their sales by six months of customer orders? Bob, overstating sales by one-half a year's customer orders is serious!" "Jennifer, this is a problem that is easy to fix. You must have Suzanne print a copy of all unshipped customer orders at each month-end closing. The total for the orders on that report will equal the correct balance in your customer deposit account." "I wonder what the year-to-date income statement will look like once I reverse out six months of sales." I responded, "Jennifer, let's get the statements right, and then we will figure out what to do. We are working on several positive changes in the shop that will increase production. Increasing shop production will increase customer orders. I hope this company is very profitable soon."

"Bob, once I finish all the monthly closes for January through July, I will print financial statements for each month and put them in two binders, one for Suzanne and one for Jonathan. As part of the monthly close package, I will write a one-page narrative highlighting what happened during the month in layperson's terms. Knowing that the two owners need to be more knowledgeable on the financial side of the business, my recap will give them a firm understanding of what the financial statements are reporting without them even reading them. After completing the financial statements and the binders, I will create the first copy of the Weekly Flash Report *(See pages #154 to #159.)* for the most recent week and file the flash reports in their binders. My next task will be to create a monthly operating budget for the balance of this year and next year. Once I complete the budget for this company and the owners approve it, and you, too, of course, I will start posting the budget on the monthly income statements with the variances.

After meeting for 15 minutes, I knew Jennifer was the right person to clean up the mess with the financial statements. She convinced me she must have had her own "Jonathan and Suzanne" at her old company. Jennifer impressed me as being intelligent, strong, and a good leader. The fact that she recently went through a sales transaction with her old company is valuable because that is Jonathan and Suzanne's goal soon. I felt fortunate that I found Jennifer so quickly for this client. She is perfect. Now, she must prove it with her work on this project.

Suzanne walked into her office to meet Jennifer and welcome her as she shook her hand. I told Suzanne that Jennifer would need some files from her to start her project. Suzanne said, "Sure, Bob, I will get her anything she needs to start." Jennifer told Suzanne she needed a username and password to log into the accounting software. She also asked for the corporation's most recent tax return and any work papers used by the tax preparer. Suzanne went to her desk and pulled a file from the bottom drawer. Then she sat down and logged in to her computer. Five minutes later,

Suzanne gave Jennifer a printout and explained, "Here is all the information you need to get into the accounting software. I went into the system files and gave you full privileges to get into any area of the software. Suzanne handed Jennifer the file with the most recent tax return and all the work papers. Jennifer reviewed the file, said thank you, and sat down at the table to get to work.

I was delighted with how Jennifer turned out. She is the perfect employee for the controller position. When I say how pleased I am with her, I should wait until I see some of her work results. But in a turnaround situation, I trust my gut with many decisions. Even if she is not as good as I expect, she is at minimal risk with this company because she is currently on a "rent to buy program," as Jonathan has classified her. When I return for my next visit in two weeks, I can tell if she is a "keeper" or, as "option #3" states, thank her for her excellent work and terminate the relationship.

*   *   *

It was now 4:00 p.m., and David was still sitting across the conference room table from me, with Jonathan on my left and Suzanne on my right. The interview started promptly at 2:00 p.m. and was supposed to end at 3.00. The first two candidates interviewed earlier for the shop supervisor position were "crash and burn" casualties. Even though they both had excellent resumes, their interview skills needed to match their resumes, and they didn't. David was materially different than the first two candidates. He was a retired military officer with solid leadership skills. David is a big guy, six foot six inches tall and 250 pounds. He has a rugged look about him. David naturally draws attention when he walks into a room because of his size and military background. Like Herman, David is an adjunct professor at WSU in their Manufacturing Engineering Technology program. David said that he knew Herman well and that he was a superstar when it came to programming those computers. David is also a computer programming course instructor and certified welder for robotic welders. The owners seemed happy with David, and he felt comfortable with Jonathan and Suzanne. During the interview, we briefly discussed compensation for the shop supervisor position without anyone having a problem with the salary amount. David said that he was satisfied with the salary for the job.

I had stopped asking questions 30 minutes ago because I was comfortable that David was the right guy to supervise the shop. Jonathan's habit of making a short story long and a long one even longer has kept David in the interview for an additional hour. What Jonathan was talking about had nothing to do with the candidate, the position, the shop, or the company. I looked at my watch because I had to get to the airport soon for my flight home. I interrupted Jonathan's unending dialogue and asked the two owners to join me in the showroom.

Once in the showroom, I asked them what they thought about David. They both agreed he was a great candidate for the shop supervisor position. I suggested we have him do a drug test, background, and credit check immediately. If he passes the tests, we should give him a copy of the job description *(See pages #125 to #127.)* and the offer letter *(See page #128.)*. I suggest offering David the job and asking him to start immediately. They both agreed with the game plan for David. Suzanne asked if I needed a ride to the airport. I said yes. Jonathan said he would give David a shop tour and get the paperwork done for his background checks.

By 4:15, Suzanne and I were in her Bronco on the way to the airport. From the time we got in the vehicle until when we arrived at the airport, Suzanne never stopped talking. Her chatting like this was unlike her since I first met her. She started by thanking me for my time and successes this week. Suzanne felt financially safe again because of all the PIRs for the business. She and Jonathan have not argued about her fear that the company will have to file for bankruptcy protection since the turnaround engagement started. Suzanne shared her insecurity because of her lack of trust in Karla's financial statements. She said they needed to know the actual status of the company's financial situation and still didn't. Suzanne said she knew they should record the customer's payments on the orders as sales only after shipping the product. She felt she had no other option with that decision, or the company would show they had lost a lot of money for several months. She said that she knew that Jonathan should not have purchased those five vehicles in the showroom. It cut their cash short and put the company at risk of being unable to make payroll. Suzanne said, "Unfortunately, Jonathan automatically goes right if I say we should go left. If I say no to a situation, he says yes and does whatever he wants.

Suzanne said Jonathan sometimes forgets that we have four kids at home and cannot afford to let this business go under. "Bob, I am so glad you are here because you are showing Jonathan how he should run this business. Jonathan has resisted taking any direction from his father, brother, or even Brian after you turned his company around to be very profitable. I can see it in his eyes that he trusts you. You do not know how glad I am that he trusts your decisions. At this point, we arrived at the airport. I jumped out of the jacked-up Bronco. I opened the backseat door and pulled out my suitcase and backpack. Suzanne had put the vehicle in park, got out, and came around to say goodbye. I was ready for her to shake my hand, but instead, she hugged me. I was surprised; this was not like the Suzanne I had known. She said, "Bob, that hug was from me and my four children at home." After that comment, I then understood what the hug was all about!

Chapter 10

WE ARE HALF WAY THERE!

"Plans are only good intentions unless they immediately degenerate into hard work."
— PETER DRUCKER – AN AUSTRAIN-AMERICAN MANAGEMENT CONSULTANT, EDUCATOR, AND AUTHOR.

Monday, September 5th – Day 7 of week 3 of the turnaround engagement

I SAT DOWN AT ONE OF THE TABLES IN THE restaurant and asked the waitress for a cup of coffee until my clients arrived. Five minutes later, Jonathan and Suzanne entered the restaurant and sat at the table. Suzanne said, "Good morning, Bob." I responded, "Good morning. How are the two of you doing?" Jonathan said, "Fine! Boy, am I hungry. Can we order our breakfast right away?" He waved the waitress over to our table. He and Suzanne ordered their regular omelet, wheat toast, and a glass of iced water. I ordered French toast and a side of ham. I asked the waitress if she could warm up my coffee.

At the beginning of this consulting engagement, we decided to have breakfast every morning to spend uninterrupted time together. The goal was to discuss what happened during the turnaround engagement and what needs to happen. So, now that the breakfast order was out of the way, I asked them how the past 12 days had gone since my last visit. Jonathan responded, "Good, Bob. How was your time at home in South Florida?" I sat there in silence and wondered what was going on. I knew Jonathan could care less about my time at home in Fort Lauderdale.

Usually, when I asked Jonathan a question, he would talk for 30 minutes without a pause. This morning was different, and I did not understand why. The waitress came and served our breakfast. There was "radio silence" from both Jonathan and Suzanne during the whole breakfast. These people are paying me a lot to make material changes to their business. When we had time together, as we had at this morning's breakfast, they should be bleeding me for information about my thoughts on how we would make their company profitable. Well, in this case, I was wrong. We all finished our breakfast and headed for the office together. For the 15-minute ride to the office, neither owner said a word. I am not insecure, but as we were traveling to the office, because of the silent treatment by both owners, there was a chance they would fire me when we got there. It was a bizarre feeling, but I visualized myself returning to the hotel, checking out, and flying home this morning. The trip to the client's offices was going in slow motion because of all the thoughts in my head about what may happen when we got to their offices.

And then it hit me; if they fired me this morning, I would be going home to my wife, the most beautiful, intelligent, kind, and loving woman on the face of the earth. I love our time together when I am home with Esther. She makes my life happy every single day. Also, when I get home, I will pull out my golf clubs and play 18 holes Tuesday morning. My mind went from 'What's *happening*?' to *'Whatever happens, I am in a good place!'*

The three of us arrived at the office and went into the showroom. The eight vehicles that were there before are gone now. There were four new pickup trucks in the middle of the room. When I saw the new trucks, I wondered why we didn't discuss this at breakfast. Jonathan said, "Bob, we were lucky; we sold all the vehicles parked in the showroom 12 days ago by posting pictures on our website and social media. We sold five in the first three days for our asking price. I visited three local dealerships when the old vehicles were out of the showroom. I got the general managers to approve us installing offroad bumpers on their brand-new pickup trucks. They even agreed to prepay for our work.

Well, my first five minutes in the showroom were extremely positive. The showroom looks great, with four dealership vehicles and no bumper parts on the floor.

Another real plus is that the company has a lot of money from selling those old vehicles in its bank account. The other wonderful issue about the company having all this cash in the bank is that they now have the funds to pay my fees. That is the thing about doing turnarounds. The clients call me because their business is losing money. The owners need to learn how to fix the problems. During a reversal, my first job is to make the business profitable. My second job is ensuring the client has enough cash in the bank to pay my invoice for my time and travel expenses. That task takes a lot of my planning and work for some clients. It requires some real effort on my part!

"Bob, I took delivery of the new vehicles one at a time. I designed and installed the new bumpers, and then we took delivery of the second vehicle. I learned my lesson to design and install one bumper at a time and not have the old parts lying everywhere in the showroom." Jonathan was extra proud of himself for selling the vehicle inventory and putting the money in their bank account. His attitude right was 180° different than it was at breakfast this morning. I am still trying to figure out what the issue was at breakfast.

After Jonathan finished telling me the stories about the sales of the vehicles and his dealing with the different general managers at the dealerships, I walked into Suzanne's office to put my backpack down. I wanted to tour the shop to see how they progressed with the relocation of each fabrication station to improve the efficiency of building the bumpers. Jonathan followed me closely into Suzanne's office like I had one-hundred-dollar bills falling out of my pockets. He said, "Go ahead, put your bag down here, and follow me to the shop. I want to show you some of our changes since your last visit." Jonathan seemed excited, just the opposite of how he was during our breakfast. I followed Jonathan out to the shop.

The first difference I noticed when we entered the shop was that it was much noisier. That had to be because much more manufacturing is happening now than a month ago. I looked around, and the place looked different, nothing like it did the last time I was here.

Jonathan had a smile on his face the size of Montana! He said, "Bob, we made some changes to the shop since your last visit. Please follow me." We walked over to the cutter. George was operating the machine. When he saw me, George walked over with a big smile. I stuck out my right hand to shake hands, and George put his arms around me and hugged me. George said, "Bob, it is great to see you. I knew it when Jonathan and Suzanne hired you; you would kick some butt and make this shop operate like a fine-tuned machine. It would be best if you saw how well this place is operating. I am so proud to be an employee of this company. A month ago, I thought we would be out of business by now. And, now we will need more shop space because business is so formidable. Bob, I am cutting steel for three times the amount of bumpers in an eight-hour shift than I was a month ago. This place is on fire. I thought I would have to look for a new job because I knew the volume we did before would not make this company profitable."

If the rest of the employees in the shop were as enthusiastic as George, I am sure he was right; this shop must be kicking butt. The new status of this shop was exciting to me, and obviously, it has Jonathan up in the clouds. We walked over to the welding robots area next. Herman was still working with these machines. I said, "Herman, I did not expect to see you still here, my friend!" With a smile, Herman said, "Mr. Curry, I am honestly having so much fun; this does not seem like work here. Jonathan and Suzanne have been wonderful to work with, and I am having difficulty leaving this place. Before I started as an instructor at the college, I worked in a shop like this one, but this company is much more friendly. Jonathan told me they have received funds from the equipment company for at least another month here, so I thought I would put in the time here and enjoy what I love doing: operating these robots." I asked if the robotic welders and grinders were all programmed for every bumper we manufacture. Herman said yes. That was great news. Herman handled all the labor required to move the front and back bumpers efficiently through the welding and grinding stations.

I asked Herman if I could review the paperwork for one of the bumpers that he was loading onto the grinder. I wanted to know the customer order date. Herman said, "Bob, the customer ordered this bumper on May 5. Today is September 5, and we are fabricating a bumper the customer ordered on May 5. That equals a 120-day order backlog. Let me say that again to myself: a "120-day" backlog. That means that within about two weeks, you have cut the backlog from six months to four. That is great news. Those robots are kicking butt with the work. Herman is the MAN!

David walked up and stuck his right hand out to shake hands. I shook his hand and welcomed him to Utah Off-road! "David, I am so glad that you are here. By a large margin, you were the best candidate for the shop supervisor position. I am so happy that you are here in control of the shop. How are things going so far? When I was here last time, I was hopeful and praying that you and Jonathan were about to shake hands on the hiring. I wanted him to hire you and get you here working as soon as possible."

David hesitated and said, "Well, Bob, when you left after my interview, Jonathan and I toured the shop. I truly wondered whether I wanted to work in a shop this disorganized. But then, Jonathan pulled out the blueprint plans for reorganizing this place. That blueprint gave me confidence when I saw it, and an hour later, Jonathan and I shook hands on a deal for me to join the company as the shop supervisor. I am teaching only one class at the university this semester, an evening class. Therefore, I was available to start the next day.

Thursday morning, I called a meeting with the whole shop staff. I gave them an "open mike" to say whatever they wanted about working here. I told them to download the problems and get them all out on the table so we could deal with them individually. That meeting, surprisingly, only lasted 15 minutes. They all talked about all the changes they have been working on since you joined the organization. They spoke of your PIRs. Bob. I have been working in a welding shop for most of my career. Until that meeting, I had no idea what "PIR" meant. After the meeting, I went to Jonathan to discuss your PIRs, and he gave me a copy of the binder you set up for him. Bob, I must tell you, I sleep with that binder every night when I go to bed. After I read it for the first time, I put together a personal task list for myself on what I wanted to accomplish each day. The action plan with all the steps listed has made my life here so much easier in this shop. I do not know how long it took you to put that binder together, but it is exactly what this place needed. Bob, you should publish this. It is valuable to every shop supervisor in any manufacturing facility worldwide. I refer to that binder as the Bible!"

Jonathan stood beside David and me, listening to our conversation and smiling. David is the answer to most of Jonathan's problems in the shop. Jonathan needs to learn how to work better with people. He would rather ignore the employees in the shop than go out there and deal with the problems to make his company profitable. David is now in charge of supervising the shop staff, which made Jonathan a happy man. He no longer must deal with those problems like the robots not working or the powder coating vendor's work sucks! Now, those are problems that David must deal with.

David offered to give me a tour of the shop to show me all the wonderful changes that they have made. I accepted his offer. David said to follow him; he wanted to start at the beginning. He wanted to start where the shop begins with a big piece of steel, cutting it into all the parts needed to manufacture an offroad bumper. We walked over to George's station, and

David explained how the paperwork flows from the customer order to a shop order. George gets the order, reviews it, and cuts a piece of steel predesigned for that bumper. George now takes the steel parts over to Herman.

A copy of the shop order goes with the bumper to the new operator of the bender, who also makes parts for the bumper and delivers them to Herman. The employee (Marcos), now operating the bender, replaced Jonathan and Suzanne's son, Bill. Bill is currently working in the accounting department with Jennifer. I heard through the grapevine that Jennifer loves working with Bill, and Bill loves working with Jennifer. That was a transfer made in heaven! Marcos was recently one of the welders, but David moved him over to the bender because of the tremendous pickup in customer orders.

Once Herman has all the pieces from the cutter and bender, he starts welding them together. This station is the "welding 1" process. After welding 1, the bumper moves to the grinder to smooth out all the rough welding spots. That grinder makes the bumper welded areas look so smooth. Next, the bumper goes to welding 2, where they add the bent pipes to the bumper. After the bumper gets through the welding 2 processes, they thoroughly inspect it. They then deliver the bumper across the street to the powder coating operation. Powder coating now takes them about two days to complete. When we bring the bumpers back here after powder coating, we inspect them thoroughly. We then pack and ship the bumpers to the customers. We now pack all the parts (screws, nuts, fasteners, bolts, and washers) in a plastic bag and tape it to the bumper. Jonathan has completed writing the installation instructions for every bumper this company manufactures. We tape the installation instructions to the bumper right next to the parts in the plastic bag.

We have created a checklist for every bumper shipment that goes out of here. That checklist follows the bumper through the whole manufacturing process. Anyone responsible for manufacturing the bumper, including the powder coating and shipping, has to initial that document. I have found that when people must put their name down that they worked on the product, they are much more careful with their work.

Bob, we are now tracking how many bumpers we ship daily, weekly, and monthly. We have created an incentive plan to compensate all the employees when they reach the monthly goal. We post the daily and weekly numbers on a board in the shop so every employee can see how they are doing and whether they are in a range to receive the monthly bonus. This past week, the shop shipped more bumpers than they did during the whole month of July. Friday afternoon, Jonathan got a case of beer and four pizzas to celebrate their success.

Last weekend, the whole group in the shop came in early Saturday morning and, as a team, reorganized all the fabrication stations as drawn on the blueprint. They all did a wonderful job and left by 1:00 p.m. This group of employees is now a team and supports each other. They are all proud of their work. Today is my eighth day here; these guys are now all part of my family. We walked over to the shipping area. Jake was busy packing a bumper. He had two guys helping him. I shook Jake's hand and asked him how things were going. David said the two young men helping Jake were from his college classes. David knew that since everything was going so well, we would need laborers to help move the products through the shop. David said he offered these two guys a temporary job at $10 per hour. They have proved to be good workers, and our shipments are staying current, even though we are shipping two or three times the number of bumpers in the past five days as we did one month ago. I introduced myself to the two guys (Jeff and Brad) and thanked them for their hard work.

I asked David how the quality of the powder coating operation was going. He answered that it was going great, no hiccups since he started eight days ago. David said they did not have to return any bumpers, and the company's turnaround time has been equal to two days. "Bob, whatever you said or threatened them with worked very well! I understand we received a free one month of their powder coating service!" I answered, "Well, David, the improved quality of the powder coating, quicker turnaround times, and a free month of their services were not negotiated by me; it was all Jonathan. Jonathan met with the company's owner while I was still in Florida and must have threatened him with finding a new company to powder coat all of our bumpers." Jonathan said, "Most of the credit should go to Bob; he was the one that wrote up the PIR about the poor powder coating quality and what we should do about it. I called the company owner at his home in Arizona. I told him we were looking for a new powder coating company because his organization is powder coating our bumpers with terrible quality. The company owner hustled up to Utah to save us as a customer. I stood there while he offered their services free for a month to save us as his customers. I would not have asked him for a month of free service; he offered it, and I shuck my head 'Yes'! All I could think of was his invoice with a big zero in the amount due column."

I congratulated David for the great start in a full sprint, which this shop needed from him. I looked David in the eyes, shook his hand, and thanked him for his impressive results.

I headed to Suzanne's office to find Jennifer and see if she had been as successful as David.

*　　*　　*

I walked out of the shop into the showroom, and Jennifer stood there with a big smile. She walked over and gave me a big hug! There must be something about people in Utah; they love to give hugs. Please don't get me wrong, I love hugging, but as a turnaround specialist, hugs seem exceedingly rare. Part of my turnaround consulting job responsibilities is to fire employees who should not be for the company. Usually, that doesn't make me the most popular person walking around the office.

Jennifer grabbed my right hand and pulled me into her office. Suzanne found the time to clean Karla's desk and freshen up the office. I sat down in the chair in front of her desk. Jennifer said that she has been looking forward to my next visit. She put a binder before me and opened it to the first page. Jennifer showed me the income statement through August 31, 20XX.

I was impressed that she had the financial statements through August, five days after the close of the month. To my surprise, the company broke even during the first eight months of the year. The income statement was cosmetically beautiful. Jennifer was proud of the work that she was showing me. I looked at the tabs in the binder: Income Statement, Balance Sheet, Monthly Narrative, Budgets, and Weekly Flash Report. Jennifer rolled her chair around her desk and sat right next to me. She moved the binder between the two of us. Jennifer wanted to walk me through all the work done and the problems in the company. Jennifer spent 30 minutes showing me everything she put together in the binder, including this year's and the next 12 months' budget.

I reviewed her work for the budgets. Her assumptions were very conservative, which is not what I had planned for this client. I want to make as many sales in the fourth quarter as this company did in the prior two quarters. That is a stretch, but it is possible because the company had less than 4% of the sales to offroad distributors like ABC Off-road Supply. There are distributors worldwide, like ABC Off-road Supply, that could easily double the sales of Utah Off-road. That could only happen if we manufacture the bumpers in two weeks and ship the order to the distributors. Now that we can manufacture the bumpers in two weeks, my job is to get customer orders.

I asked Jennifer about how Bill was doing working for her. She said, "Bob, I am having a wonderful time working with that young gentleman. When I give him an assignment, he goes off and gets it done. He has never once asked me to show him what to do. If he does not understand what I am asking, he researches and completes the project. He has had an accounting course or two in high school and has a firm accounting foundation for a high school student. I have never met such a mature young man. Jonathan and Suzanne should be proud of Bill. I know I am, and I have only known him for about two weeks.

I thanked Jennifer for her time and wonderful work with the financial statements. She did an impressive job in a brief period.

Chapter 11

"AND NOW YOU KNOW...THE REST OF THE STORY!"

"Employees who believe that management is concerned about them as a whole person – not just an employee – are more productive, more satisfied, more fulfilled. Satisfied employees mean satisfied customers, which leads to profitability."
— ANNE M. MULCAHY – THE FORMER CHAIRPERSON AND CEO OF XEROX CORPORATION.

Wednesday, January 4th – Day 36 of week 12 of the turnaround engagement

MY FLIGHT HOME TONIGHT TO FORT LAUDERDALE is taking off at 7:15 p.m., so I had to have my luggage packed this morning and check out of the hotel. I will not have to return to Utah again in another two weeks because the turnaround engagement is 99% done as far as I am concerned. At 7:45 a.m., I went downstairs to check out and get some breakfast. When I walked into the restaurant, much to my surprise, Jonathan and Suzanne were sitting at a table, ready to order breakfast. When I arrived at their table, Jonathan stood to shake my hand and welcomed me to breakfast. After coming to Utah every other week for four months and meeting the owners for breakfast every morning, they finally beat me to the breakfast table. I told Jonathan, "You don't need to stand up; It's only me." Jonathan laughed; we shook hands, and both sat down. By then, the waitress stood beside us, ready to take our order. I asked Suzanne why they were at the restaurant so early today. They were here 15 minutes before we agreed to meet and half an hour earlier than their usual arrival time. Normally, they are 20 minutes late. She said, "Bob, our kids don't have school today, so I did not have to get up, pack lunches, and drive them to school. So, Jonathan and I were up and ready to leave the house at 7:30. We arrived here at 7:45. I must tell you, it felt different this morning, showing up here 15 minutes early rather than 20 minutes late as usual."

Right then, the three of us ordered breakfast. Jonathan pulled a notebook out of his backpack and set it in front of him. He said, "Bob, this will likely be your last day for this turnaround engagement. Is that accurate?" I shook my head yes to agree with him. He continued, "I have much to say to you, and I didn't want to forget anything. I wrote down my thoughts in my notebook." I just sat there and listened because I had no idea what Jonathan would say.

Jonathan opened his notebook and started,

Thank you - "First, and probably most importantly, Suzanne and I want to thank you for what you have done for our company. Your consulting services have saved our business from eventually filing for bankruptcy. If you did not come here when you did, there is no doubt in my mind that we would not have been in business today. Your vision of how to run a business, this business, has taught me a lot. Bob, I am sure you know it is much easier to manage a profitable business with positive cash flow and has more orders than we have ever had in the company's history."

Hire the Best! – "You hired five new employees, four of them from *WSU* (David, Herman, Jeff, and Brad). And then you found Jennifer at *B2BCPA*, who may be the absolute best employee we have ever had in the history of this company. It is easier to run a company with an excellent controller who manages an accounting department. For once in the history of this company, we know our financial information is accurate."

Recruiting and Hiring – "You took charge here by recruiting and hiring Jennifer and David. You hand-picked our controller and shop supervisor, ensuring we hired the right people."

Robotic Machines and Herman – "You saw I had done nothing to get the four robotic machines in the shop programmed. That was hurting our business. When we hired Herman, his programming did miracles to produce the bumpers. He and those machines have lowered the order backlog from 26 weeks to three weeks in two months."

"Herman came to me last night after work and asked me if I was interested in hiring him full-time to work in the shop. I am just talking to you now about it because I know what you think about him and his skills. I knew you would strongly recommend offering him a full-time position with the organization."

"We also discussed starting our internship program with WSU during the second week of January. I asked Herman if he would be interested in managing the program. The three interns would report directly to him in the shop. Herman loved managing those three students, which will elevate his position with the company. That way, I can pay him a higher salary. He also liked the idea, especially about the higher salary."

Installation Instructions – "You recognized that we were not shipping installation instructions with the bumpers, which was a major problem. It was causing our customer base to be truly angry with our company. You are responsible for lighting a fire under my butt to write the instructions. Your unique way of lighting fires in certain places motivates people, especially me! Honestly, I did not want to be on your wrong side when you were doing such a great job with the rest of the company."

Our waitress served our breakfast and warmed up my coffee. By this time, Jonathan was so excited about what he was talking about that he almost did not notice that his breakfast was in front of him. I kept interrupting Jonathan for the next hour, reminding him to eat.

Clean the showroom, offices, shop, and bathrooms – "You made it very clear that we were not maintaining the offices, showroom, bathrooms, and shop. You said this place looks like a city dump. We would have never been able to hire Jennifer, David, or Herman if we had not cleaned this place. These three classy executives we hired would have never agreed to come here if this place still looked like the city dump."

Fix powder coating vendor – "Our powder coating vendor did a poor job coating our bumpers. You lit another fire under my butt. I met with the company's owner and immediately resolved the problem. Plus, we got a month's worth of our bumpers powder coated for free."

Terminating poor performing employee – "Because of our old hiring philosophy, we settled with the poor performance by Karla with our financial statements. You suggested that we terminate Karla, which we did. Now we have Jennifer, whom I call "the company superstar!" She supplies us with Weekly Flash Reports, Monthly Income Statements with budgets, and Balance Sheets. We get the flash reports every Monday and the financial statements by the tenth of every month.

Transfer Bill from shop to accounting department – "We also want to thank you for recommending that we move Bill, our son, out of the shop and work for Jennifer in the accounting department. As it turns out, Bill loves working there and has decided to major in business in college next year rather than computer programming."

"Suzanne and I will celebrate when Bill graduates college with a business degree. He will be the first person in our family to have any education in business."

Managing the business – "Jennifer and David now run our company like a professional organization. Jennifer's financial reporting is second to none. The financial statements that she produces for us are timely and accurate. Her narratives of the monthly activity are extremely valuable to Suzanne and me."

"She gets here early every morning, sits at her desk, and works non-stop all day. She prepares all the invoices with the checks attached for Suzanne to sign. She has all the accounts receivables collected and current. She renegotiated our property and liability insurance with our insurance broker and saved the company a lot of money because of a 25% reduction in our premiums. She has worked with David to create operational reporting for him on the daily shipments of bumpers to our customers."

"Two weeks ago, Jennifer sent me a worksheet with an annual budget for this new year. Once I reviewed it, I returned the budget to her. I told her to plan for an increase in the total sales for the year by 250% over last year's revenue. Since our fourth quarter revenue was equal to the second and third quarters combined, I thought our plan for next year's sales must be much larger."

Less stress – "Bob, when you started here, I was so stressed that I could not stay at the office many days and work a full day. Now, I am feeling zero stress. I now enjoy coming to work. In the past four months, I have learned that it is easy to relax during the eight hours at work because I have David supervising the shop and Herman kicking butt with the four robots. Jennifer, Herman, and David have been amazing additions to the team. They are all "A" players in my eyes."

Employee turnover – "Mr. Curry, before you started, the turnover of our shop employees was ridiculous. We have not had an employee give notice and leave since the beginning of August."

Production incentive plan – "During the fourth quarter, we have paid incentive bonuses to all the shop workers because they exceeded their shipping goals. Actually, they blew them out of the water. By November 1st, our customer order backlog was down from 26 weeks in August to three weeks on October 31st."

Marketing plan to sell to distributors – "Once the company got the order backlog down to three weeks, we started a direct marketing plan to all the distributorships in the United States. During December, the shop hit its shipping goal by December 15th with two more weeks of shipping bumpers until the end of the month. There are now many distributorships selling our products, like ABC Off-road Supply. Our marketing focus is to inform all distributors that we ship our bumpers two weeks after receiving the customer orders. We put banners across our website with the message: "We ship our orders

in two weeks after we receive the order from the customer."
We put the same message on all our social media sites. The
marketing made our phones ring, and we received customer
orders almost 24 hours daily."

Sales growth – "December was the largest month
for sales in the company's history for customer orders and
shipments. When you put those two statistics together, we
manufactured more bumpers in December than any other
month since Suzanne and I started the company. With the
huge jump in sales, Suzanne and I were concerned that it
would put major stress on our employees in the shop. Well,
my assumption was not accurate. The sales growth excited
the whole group because they knew that the more bumpers
they manufactured and shipped, the more money they would
make with their bonus plan. The more orders we received,
the more bumpers they manufactured. The major growth in
sales was not a problem with our team in the shop, thanks
to how well David supervises that group."

Weber State University – "Your idea about hiring
people from WSU was a wonderful suggestion. I have learned
loads from all the new hires (David, Herman, Jeff, and Brad).
Hiring Jeff and Brad, two young men out of college, has
worked out very well. They are both intelligent, hardworking,
and ambitious. Those two young men plan to learn the skills
at each of the shop's stations, how to run all the equipment,
and how to manage the shop staff. I have talked to them
several times over the past couple of months. They both
said their career goal is to be a shop supervisor like David
in a few years. After they get the experience supervising the
shop, they want to start their own manufacturing business.
These two kids are only 20 years old and have the maturity

level of a 40-year-old professional. Working with people who have their future mapped out is a pleasure."

Jonathan finished his list of what he wanted to discuss this morning and at breakfast. The waitress brought over our check, I signed it, and we headed to the office.

*　　*　　*

I sat down at the conference room table in Suzanne's office to tie up some loose ends before I flew home later. Jennifer came in, wished me 'Good Morning,' and handed me her binder. She said, "Bob, look at the December numbers and the year-to-date profit." I opened the binder and could not believe that this company made a $330,000 profit for the year. As of the end of August, this company was at breakeven for the year-to-date income statement. Jennifer said, "Bob, that profit was made mostly in December because of our amazing monthly shipments. If we keep manufacturing and shipping at this rate, this company will report a profit of at least $3,000,000 next year. How exciting is that?" My answer was, "REAL EXCITING!" I asked Jennifer to find Jonathan and Suzanne and ask them to review your exciting financial reports.

Jonathan, Suzanne, Jennifer, and I sat at the table two minutes later. Jennifer got the owner's financial statement binders and brought them to our meeting. I will let Jennifer explain the December and year-to-date numbers to the owners, plus her budget projections for next year's profit. The look on their faces was complete excitement. Jonathan asked me, "Bob, I assume you are confirming Jennifer's December income statement for this year and next year's projections."

I smiled and answered, "Yes, I am!" I confirmed her work because I reviewed her general ledger analysis yesterday.

Olivia walked into Suzanne's office from the customer service department and said, "Excuse me, Jonathan, but you have three surprise visitors out front. They said they were in the area and wanted to stop in and wish you and Suzanne a Happy New Year." Jonathan asked her, "Who is it? We are really busy here." Olivia answered, "It's Noah and his two brothers, Mark and Peter." Jonathan jumped out of his chair and went out front to greet them. A minute later, the three brothers and Jonathan came back into the office, and all sat at the table after I shook hands with each of the three brothers. I introduced Jennifer to Noah, Mark, and Peter and told her who they were.

Noah said, "Bob, I am surprised you are still here. How much longer are you planning to be here?" I told him that today was my last day, and I was flying home this evening. "So, how did the turnaround go? Were you able to pound in any business sense into Jonathan's brain while you were here?" I said that I would let Jonathan answer his question. Jonathan said, "Noah, I am unsure how to answer your question. This year, we made about one-third of a million dollars in profits for the fourth quarter. My excellent controller, Jennifer, is projecting for the budget next year, we should make a pre-tax profit of $3,000,000. Noah's face turned red when he heard about next year's profit projections. Noah asked me, "Bob, do you agree with those figures?" I looked at Jonathan to see if he permitted me to answer Noah's questions. Jonathan smiled and shook his head yes. "Noah, I do agree with the profits for the past year. The actual number was $330,000 year-to-date. We have the best controller in the state of Utah reporting them. Jennifer looked at me with a big smile.

Regarding next year's projections, I'm afraid I have to disagree. My good friend Jennifer is slightly conservative with her sales and profits forecasts. If this company makes $3,000,000 next year, I would be pleased but not overly impressed. Our budget calls for a 250% growth in sales. Sales will range from 300% to 350% growth. This past December's sales were equal to last year's total sales during the first quarter."

Jonathan looked at Noah with a serious look and asked, "Are you still interested in buying my company, Noah? If you are, make us an offer, and I will give you an answer soon." Jonathan looked at me with a big smile and said, "Bob, do you remember the subject matter in PIR #2?" I said that I did! I was proud of Jonathan; he took this consulting engagement seriously and learned a lot. Noah said, "Jonathan, would you sell the company for the price we discussed four months ago, $10,000,000?" Jonathan answered, "Noah, let me get with Suzanne and Bob, and I will get back to you with my answer. Jonathan looked at Suzanne and then stared at me about how he was going to respond to Noah's offer. He said, "Noah, no, that is not close to this company's value. I am not going to sell. I will hang around here and use the business sense that Bob pounded into my brain and see what the company looks like in the next 12 months."

Noah stood up and wished everyone a Happy New Year. He and his two brothers left Suzanne's office without saying another word. Once Noah and his brothers were gone, Jonathan looked at me and said, "You have no idea how good it felt to turn down his offer. It felt wonderful. I love being in a position of power with that guy!"

At 4:00 p.m., Suzanne rode me to the airport and dropped me off for my flight home. On the way to the airport,

Suzanne said, "Bob, I want to thank you for what you have done for our company. More importantly, thank you for what you have done to destress Jonathan."

Just as Paul Harvey used to say at the end of his radio broadcasts, "*And Now you know…THE REST of the story!*"

About the Author

Robert S. ("Bob") Curry is an author, a seasoned business coach, and a successful turnaround specialist with over 25 years of experience. Bob has had great success with turning around companies as small as $3,000,000 and as large as $1,300,000,000. Early in his career, he served as a public accountant for two years before taking on the roles of controller, CFO, and president/CEO. Bob started his turnaround career as president/CEO of three companies— all of which experienced successful turnarounds under his direction. In the late 1990s, he began his turnaround consulting firm, and for the past 25 years, he has worked with more than 80 companies, helping each to establish a strong management team and become profitable. He resides in Fort Lauderdale, Florida, with his wife, Esther.

www.ingramcontent.com/pod-product-compliance
Lightning Source LLC
Chambersburg PA
CBHW051244020426
42333CB00025B/3050